Doug Harris has compiled, through a [...] excellent, in depth study of the Jehova[...] be of great value to the average church [...] than just shut the door abruptly in the [...] ing on their doorstep.

The Jehovah's Witnesses – Their Beliefs & Practices is a timely warning for church leaders to beware of their doctrines and the way in which they can so easily infiltrate and influence mainstream Christianity. It is also an invaluable resource for students of the Bible to research further, the dangers and difficulties, which arise for individuals and society as a result of associating the beliefs and practices of the Witnesses.

The fact of the matter is that it is vitally important that we understand the Witnesses, not to judge or argue more vehemently, but to become more confident in sharing with them the real Jesus Christ. My prayer is that through this book, many will catch the vision to do so when next facing a Jehovah's Witness on the doorstep.

Dave Edwins, Head of Evangelism, Moorlands Bible College

Doug Harris sets out with grace and integrity, to help Christians understand the Jehovah's Witnesses so that they can engage them with confidence and effectiveness. The hope is that they will be helped and not condemned in their search for the truth.

This is a detailed but accessible book which will be of great interest to students, local church leaders and any Christians who have a real concern for all who are caught up in the erroneous doctrines of the Jehovah's Witnesses.

Paul Harris, Head of Evangelism, Evangelical Alliance

If the ordinary Jehovah's Witness is expected to spend 10 hours a week delivering Watchtower teaching, it shouldn't be too much to ask ordinary Christians to spend 10 hours in a lifetime to get to grips with the history and beliefs of the Jehovah's Witnesses so that the Christian can offer in depth help.

It's all here! Comprehensive and incisive. History, doctrine and practice, analysis and comment. *This book makes the challenge do-able.* Doug Harris's immense knowledge and spiritual perception are harnessed to unmask the pitfalls of Jehovah's Witnesses. Any who know him, will also appreciate his passion to see people brought into freedom as children of God.

Rev. Dr. David Spriggs BA

Doug Harris is married with three children and has been a Christian since 1963. In 1981 after watching hundreds of Jehovah's Witnesses going to their convention in Twickenham, he was challenged to get involved in reaching out to all those involved in the Watchtower Society.

During the last seventeen years the work of Reachout Trust has grown from a local outreach to one group, to an international work which has now become recognised for its endeavours to reach out to all who are involved in the cults, occult, new age and to any non biblical teaching practices. In 1998 Reachout Trust had over 12,000 enquiries from people requesting help.

Each year Doug Harris conducts more than 100 seminars to inform and train others to become involved in this work. He also undertakes many TV and Radio interviews and is an author of a number of books on the subject of the cults.

THE JEHOVAH'S WITNESSES

THEIR BELIEFS AND PRACTICES

Doug Harris

Gazelle
BOOKS

MILL HILL, LONDON NW7 3SA

Original edition first published 1988
and reprinted in 1993 titled *Awake! To The Watchtower*.

This revised and expanded edition published 1999
by Gazelle Books, Concorde House, Grenville Place,
Mill Hill, London NW7 3SA.

ISBN 1 899746 13 7

Designed and Produced for
GAZELLE BOOKS
in association with Reachout Trust
by Gazelle Creative Productions Ltd,
Concorde House, Grenville Place, Mill Hill, London NW7 3SA.

CONTENTS

Introduction

Welcome to this revised and expanded version of *The Jehovah's Witnesses – their beliefs and practices*. We have been delighted by the way the Lord has used the previous editions and we trust that this one will continue to be used in helping Christians and Jehovah's Witnesses alike; Christians to see that they can witness and Jehovah's Witnesses to find the truth.

Those who have seen previous editions will notice some new aspects to this edition as we have sought to make it more 'user-friendly'. I must thank the many people who have sent in suggestions or those who even just sparked off a thought in conversation. Special thanks need to go to Bill Browning who had a large input into the previous edition, some of which has survived into this more-streamlined publication.

Additional study material
For those who want to study in more depth, extended material and resources are available on page 203 and in the Appendices at the back of this book.

Long quotations
For space reasons, we have not printed out every quote from *The Watchtower* or other Jehovah's Witness books. Photocopies of most if not all of these are available from Reachout Trust. Depending on quantity, they will cost between 7p and 10p per copy plus postage. Please contact the Richmond Office for details of availability and costs, quoting the full title of the copy wanted and the page number of *The Jehovah's Witnesses* that it is quoted on.

Reachout Trust
Reachout Trust is a ministry that wants to help you put into practice the suggestions made in this book. Details of some of

the ways we can do this and also some of the ways you can help us are given at the end of the book. Appendix B lists some further resources that you may find useful, which can be obtained from the Trust.

If you are or have been involved with the Watchtower Bible & Tract Society you might have questions arising out of this book and either want help in answering them or indeed help to leave the Society. We would be glad to help in the way best for you; please write, fax or e-mail us to the address below. We would be happy, if you desire, to arrange for you to talk to someone near you. This would be in strictest confidence.

If you want to help others you might like to consider arranging an in-depth seminar at your church. Alternatively, maybe one of our training videos would help you spread the message that it is worthwhile and possible to talk to Jehovah's Witnesses. At the very least please write and ask for our detailed information pack so that you can consider these matters further.

If you have a burden for this work, you might want to consider becoming one of our team members. Full details for applying for this will be found at the end of the book.

Please do not hesitate to contact us should you need anything further.

Doug Harris   January 1999
Reachout Trust
24 Ormond Road
Richmond
Surrey TW10 6TH
Tel: 0181 332 7785
Fax: 0181 332 0286
E-mail: doug@reachouttrust.org

NOTES

Explanations

To help you get the most out of this book and understand its layout it is important for you to read this section.

Quotations

Italics within quotations occur in the original, and may indicate emphasis or the use of a transliterated Hebrew or Greek word.

SMALL CAPITAL LETTERS indicate our emphasis.

Bold print indicates the reinsertion of words that the Watchtower has replaced by '...'

Abbreviations used

Aw. – *Awake!*, WBTS, various editions

CE – *Common Era*

EA – *Encyclopaedia Americana*, various editions

EB – *Encyclopaedia Britannica*, various editions

Insight – *Insight on the Scriptures*, WBTS, 1988

KIT – *Kingdom Interlinear Translation of the Greek Scriptures*, WBTS, 1969 & 1985

NCE – *New Catholic Encyclopaedia*, various editions

NWT – *New World Translation of the Scriptures*, WBTS, various editions

Reasoning – *Reasoning from the Scriptures*, WBTS, 1985

Vine – *Expository Dictionary of New Testament Words*, W. E. Vine, 1966

WBTS – Watchtower Bible & Tract Society

WT – *The Watchtower*, various editions

WTR – *The Watch Tower Reprints*, various editions

YB – *Yearbook of Jehovah's Witnesses*, various editions

ZWTR – *Zion's Watch Tower Reprints*, various editions

Glossary of terms

Awake! – one of the twice-monthly magazines of the Jehovah's Witnesses

Faithful and Discreet Slave, the – title Jehovah's Witnesses give to those who lead the WBTS

Governing Body – name for the group of men who run the WBTS

Kingdom Hall – name given to a Jehovah's Witness meeting place

Overseer – a man who has a specific responsibility in a local congregation of Jehovah's Witnesses

Organisation, the – see Watchtower Organisation

Publisher, – every Jehovah's Witness is called this because they publish the good news of the Kingdom

Society, the – shortened form of the Watchtower Bible & Tract Society

Watchtower Bible & Tract Society, the – the official name for the Jehovah's Witnesses

Watchtower Organisation, the – see Watchtower Bible & Tract Society

Watchtower, The – one of the twice-monthly magazines of the Jehovah's Witnesses

1

The Christian Witness

— ❧ —

This chapter gives an overview of the basics for sharing our faith with a Jehovah's Witness. What we present here in seed form will, we trust, grow into full blossom by the end of the book.

Although this book is primarily about Jehovah's Witnesses, we cannot begin there. We must begin with ourselves; our attitude and our motivation. Maybe there is even a step before this – what does the Lord think about Jehovah's Witnesses and how does He view them?

John 3:16 confirms that God loves the world, which includes Jehovah's Witnesses. The Lord longs for them to be saved. If it were possible for God to love one group more than another, I believe He would choose Witnesses and others like them. Those who often have reached out for God and spiritual things but have been misled and deceived into a man-made religion.

Christians have a God-given commission to share the gospel with Jehovah's Witnesses but often because of fear or ignorance we turn a 'deaf ear' and hope they go away. We should also add here that some feel they have a Biblical reason for not talking to members of cults.

For example, can 2 John 10 be used in such a way? I do not believe it can. Verse 7 shows us that the context is those who were in the church but have left (see also 1 John 2:19). The church knew these people had deliberately rejected the truth. This is not the case with the majority of Jehovah's Witnesses;

they have not had the opportunity to hear the truth in a way they understand.

I believe also that we need to put these verses into the context of the whole New Testament. The longing of God's heart for all to be saved and the sacrifice of Jesus Christ for the whole world. This includes Jehovah's Witnesses. It is possible that there are a small minority of Witnesses that fit the description in these verses but I would say that 99% of those you meet do not. These are the ones that have reached out for God and salvation but they were deceived with a false gospel. What an opportunity we have!

Can we learn anything from these verses then? I believe we should be careful that there are no 'weak' or young Christians present, who might be caused to stumble, when we talk with the Witness. Also that we should not allow them to speak publicly in a meeting if there are those who could be adversely affected. Apart from this let us do all we can to reach out to these ones and love them to a true relationship with Jesus.

Our desire is that this book will help overcome these and any other negative feelings you may have towards the Witnesses. The Jehovah's Witness comes with a false gospel and in so doing asks, 'Why do you believe differently?' The worse thing we can do is 'persecute' them by setting free the dog or slamming the door in their face. All that will do, is confirm to them that they are 'in the truth!'

1 Pet. 3:15 tells of Christ's promise to help us give an effective answer if He has the central place in our lives. It may not be a theological discourse, probably better not, but it will be a clear word of testimony of the real Christ. We are also told that this answer should be with gentleness and reverence! Gentleness towards the person and reverence towards God.

The right motivation

Three words should sum up our motivation, love, love and love! The desire of the Lord's heart is to rescue these ones and to this, we should willingly sacrifice our time and talents. If this is a problem to you please meditate on John 3:16-17, especially verse 17; Rom. 9:1-3,10:1-3; and 2 Pet. 3:8-9. See the motivation of those mentioned. Christ came to this world because of love; Paul reached out to those who hated him because of love; Christ has not returned to this world yet because He loves all and wants all to be saved. This alone should be our motivation: I love Jehovah's Witnesses and I want to see them free in Christ.

An essential passage to help us is John 4. Note carefully how Jesus treated the Samaritan woman. He knew she was a 'Samaritan adulteress' but He did not just wildly accuse her, instead He built a bridge of love and trust. Because of His love, the woman and the whole village heard about Jesus. If He had condemned her, it would have been a very different story

Importance of Prayer
We are at war, but as Eph. 6:12 clearly shows us, it is not with the Jehovah's Witness but with the spiritual forces behind the Society (see also 2 Cor. 4:1-4). We need to learn to fight in this Spiritual battle. When David went out against Goliath, he would not use Saul's armour because he had not tested it. (1 Sam. 17:31-40) As with David, now, before we get into the battle, is the time to learn to trust God and to learn to use His weapons. The battlefield is no place for experimentation.

We can also learn from Jehoshophat in 2 Chron. 20. When the army surrounded him (v 1) the Scripture clearly says that he was afraid (v 3a). Yet, see what happens when he calls the people to pray and fast (v 3b) and reminds them of the sovereignty of the Lord (v 6). God speaks and deals with the fear (v 15) and gives victory (v 17). Do not be concerned about initial fear but handle it in the right way.

Confidence in the Word of God
There is no substitute for this. We need a basic grasp of our own doctrines, salvation, justification, sanctification, hell, eternal life, etc. The reason the Witness often stumps us is that we do

not know what we believe and therefore we cannot argue that they are wrong! Let's get stuck in or, as one brother says, 'thou shalt bash on!' (See John 5:39,17:3; Matt. 16:13-16).

Understanding the Jehovah's Witnesses

To talk at depth with a Witness you will need to know something about them. This is what this book is about. We need to know what are sensitive subjects and how to deal with them. We are to initially accept the Witnesses as they are and build bridges, not make a kamikaze run. In our first contact it is usually best to avoid areas that provoke hostility, for example, the Trinity, blood, the cross or stake, Christmas. All these subjects can be dealt with later but they are not the best for bridge building.

How to present yourself

When time permits, three basic areas should be presented to the Witness. First, sow doubts about the Watchtower organisation by asking questions and not by accusation. Second, present clearly the person of Jesus Christ. Third, show what their relationship needs to be to Jesus. Never just present the first area and leave it there. What is the point of cataloguing the faults of a sinking ship? Throw a lifebelt! Remember too that when you sow doubts about the organisation do so in a loving way; never be vindictive or spiteful. Where possible have Watchtower literature or at least the date and page of statements you wish to quote so that the matter can be established.

The following pages will provide material for you to come to know the errors of the organisation, and how to share positively the gospel of our Lord Jesus. Happy reading!

2

The Historical Background

___ ⟲ ___

As I understand it, it is very unlikely that Charles Taze Russell actually set out to create what today is known as the WBTS. Even if he did, his version is certainly not the one we have now. If Russell were alive today, he would be disfellowshipped because so many changes have taken place over the years.

Founder and First President – Charles Taze Russell

Charles Taze Russell was born 16 February 1852 in Allegheny City, Pennsylvania to Presbyterian parents. He joined the Congregational Church but by the time he reached his late teens, he rejected most of the 'Christian' influence and studied Buddhism, Confucianism and other Oriental religions.

Russell only had elementary education, which would probably not have helped him in the study of Greek and Hebrew, something that would appear necessary for some of the claims he made in later life. Probably the most famous was made in a libel case where he was questioned about his scholastic standing. On the stand, he admitted that he had left school at fourteen after only seven years tuition. He was then questioned as follows:

Q. 'Do you know the Greek alphabet?'
A. 'Oh yes.'
Q. 'Can you tell me the correct letters if you see them?'
A. 'Some of them, I might make a mistake on some of them.'
Q. 'Would you tell me the names of those on top of the page, page 447 I have got here?'

A. 'Well I don't know that I would be able to.'

Q. 'You can't tell what those letters are, look at them and see if you know?'

A. 'My way. . .' (he was interrupted at this point and not allowed to explain)

Q. 'Are you familiar with the Greek language?'

A. 'No.'

There is no doubt that the interruption was a typical 'attorney' ploy that we have all seen, at least on television. What Russell was not allowed to say when he was interrupted was that he had developed a schoolboy's ability to recognise Greek words in Strong's and Young's Concordances. We make this point because the purpose of citing this quote is not to defame Russell in anyway but to conclude, from our point of view, that such a man would not have the qualifications needed to develop doctrines on the meanings of various words as he did. In the same trial he also went on to admit that he didn't know Hebrew and so the same would be true of the Old Testament.

The search begins

In 1870 Russell came under the influence of the Second Adventists and especially the teachings of William Miller. (More will be said of this when we look at Watchtower chronology.)

> Among other theories, I stumbled upon Adventism. Seemingly by accident, one evening I dropped into a dusty, dingy hall, where I had heard religious services were held, to see if the handful who met there had anything more sensible to offer than the creeds of the great churches. There, for the first time, I heard something of the views of Second Adventists, the preacher being Mr. Jonas Wendell, long since deceased. Thus I confess my indebtedness to Adventists as well as to other denominations. (*ZWTR*, 15 July 1906, p. 3821)

Affected by what he heard he and six others started a home Bible study to investigate further the things they were hearing about. The study led to Russell's first booklet being published. Entitled *The Object and Manner of the Lord's Return*, it concluded that the Lord's return would be invisible.

This first booklet has caused the Watchtower historians some problems, something that would be repeated with other of Russell's writings. The problem is, when was it published? The title page of the publication and the 1949 *Watchtower* show that Russell wrote this pamphlet in 1877.

> Well, then, in the spring of 1877, or over two years before starting this magazine, the said Russell published a pamphlet entitled 'The Object and Manner of the Lord's Return' – *WT*, 1 July 1949.

However, the Society's 'official' history in 1975 changed the date of the publication to 1873.

> Earnestly endeavouring to counteract such erroneous teachings, in 1873 twenty-one-year-old C. T. Russell wrote and published at his own expense a booklet entitled 'The Object and Manner of the Lord's Return'. Some 50,000 copies were published and it enjoyed a wide distribution. About January of 1876, Russell received a copy of the religious periodical *The Herald of the Morning* – *YB*, 1975, p. 36.

Why the change? The following quotation gives the clue.

> Looking back to 1871, we see that many of our company were what are known as Second Adventists, and the light they held briefly stated, was that there would be a second advent of Jesus ... This, they claimed would occur in 1873 ... Well, 1873 came, the end of 6000 years, and yet no burning of the world. – *ZWTR*, February 1881, p. 188.

In 1874 Russell was looking for the 'visible' return of Christ. The 'visible' was only changed to the 'invisible' when the event did not happen. By changing the publication date to 1873 the Society makes Russell appear to be a 'prophet' of Christ's invisible return (albeit forty years earlier than the Society now believes) whereas in reality he was a false prophet covering another error.

The Society's latest 'official' history book, *Jehovah's Witnesses Proclaiming God's Kingdom*, now contradicts its original statement and confirms on p. 47 that publication date was 1877. This small incident shows the ability the Society has to change its own history and indeed that its founder was looking for the visible return of the Lord as late as 1877!

That Russell was still looking for the visible return of the Lord is shown by the book he co-published with N. H. Barbour, *Three Worlds and the Harvest of the World*. Although this mainly seems to be the work of Barbour, Russell was glad to add his name to it and therefore accept the teaching included that the saints would be 'caught away bodily' in 1878.

> Hence, if he is to COME TO harvest the EARTH, to gather his saints; and is also to come 'with all his saints'; there must be two parts or stages of his coming ... The harvest is a definite period of time ... And yet the LIVING SAINTS ARE NOT TAKEN UNTIL NEAR THE END OF THE HARVEST ... the harvest ... began on the tenth day of the seventh month in 1874. And ... measures three and a half years. – *Three Worlds or Plan of Redemption*, 1877, N. H. Barbour and C. T. Russell, pp. 28-30.

When this didn't happen, Russell made the first major U-turn of the Society, explaining that the resurrection of the dead began in 1878 and that all Christians dying after then would go straight to be with the Lord. Even this explanation has since been changed by the Society and so we can see clear evidence of the confusion of dates at the beginning of the history of the WBTS.

It was evident, then, that though the manner in which they had expected Jesus was in error, yet the time, as indicated by the 'Midnight Cry', was correct, and that the Bridegroom came in the Autumn of 1874 ... If these movements were of God, and if Bros. Miller and Barbour were his instruments, then that 'Midnight Cry', based on the prophetic and other statements and evidences, was correct, and the 'Bridegroom came' in 1874. We believe that Midnight Cry was of God, and was fulfilled by the Bridegroom's coming, not because Bros. Miller and Barbour claimed it, but because the Word of God supports it. (*ZWTR*, October/November 1881, p. 289)

Date setting and changing

What many modern Jehovah's Witnesses do not know is even what they believe about dates today is not what Russell taught at the beginning.

> ... when Charles Taze Russell began publishing his own religious magazine in July of 1879, he published it under the title *Zion's Watch Tower and Herald of Christ's Presence*. He had already become familiar with Wilson's *The Emphatic Diaglott*, which translated the Greek word *parousia* as 'presence', not 'coming', in Matthew 24:3 and elsewhere. The new magazine was heralding Christ's invisible presence as having begun in 1874. This presence was to continue until the end of the Gentile Times in 1914, when the Gentile nations would be destroyed and the remnant of the 'chaste virgin' class would be glorified with their bridegroom in heaven by death and resurrection to life in the spirit. (*God's Kingdom of a 1,000 years has Approached*, WBTS, 1973, pp. 187-188)

God's absolute dates cannot be changed and yet the Society has changed and altered editions of books to reflect the 'changing God' it believes in. The following change gives an example of this:

'... and the full establishment of the Kingdom of God in the earth at AD 1914, the terminus of the Times of the Gentiles.' (*The Time is at Hand*, WBTS, 1888 edition, p. 126)

'... and the full establishment of the Kingdom of God in the earth AFTER AD 1914, the terminus of the Times of the Gentiles.' (*The Time is at Hand*, WBTS, 1925 edition, p. 126)

Even methods that Russell used to establish God's dates are now seen as 'Satanic'

> The Great Pyramid ... a storehouse of truth, scientific, historic and prophetic-Bible allusions to it. (The Time is at Hand, WBTS, 1891, p. 17)
>
> If the pyramid is not mentioned in the Bible, then following its teachings is being led by vain philosophy and false science and not following after Christ ... Then Satan put his knowledge in dead stone, which may be called Satan's Bible, and not God's stone witness. (WT, 15 November 1928, pp. 341,344)

The Watchtower

In July 1879, 6000 copies of the first issue of the then-entitled *Zion's Watch Tower and Herald of Christ's Presence* were printed. In the same year, Russell married Maria F. Ackley, an event destined not to last as long as the *Watchtower*. Maria left him in 1897 and a legal separation took place in 1908. The judge concluded that the way Russell treated his wife 'would necessarily render the life of any sensitive Christian woman a burden and make her conditions intolerable.' Other accusations have been made against Russell including child molesting, and his personal life certainly is a chequered history. Yet through it all the Society continued to grow with the Watchtower Bible and Tract Society being formed in 1881 and incorporated in 1884.

Russell's writings also developed both in book form and

through the pages of The Watchtower. In 1886 Volume 1 of the *Millennial Dawn* was published (today it is known as *Studies in the Scriptures*). Russell would write five other volumes and came to consider them as more important than the Bible.

> Furthermore, not only do we find that people cannot see the divine plan in studying the Bible by itself, but we see, also, that if anyone lays the SCRIPTURE STUDIES aside, even after he has used them, after he has become familiar with them, after he has read them for ten years-if he then lays them aside and ignores them and goes to the Bible alone, though he has understood his Bible for ten years, our experience shows that within two years he goes into darkness. On the other hand, if he had merely read the SCRIPTURE STUDIES with their references, and had not read a page of the Bible, as such, he would be in the light at the end of two years, because he would have the light of the Scriptures. (*WTR*, 15 September 1910, p. 4685)

It was not just these six volumes that got Russell into hot water, some of the stories recorded in *The Watchtower* were also held up to ridicule. Desiring to show that the 'return of Christ' was near Russell wanted to show that 'things were happening' in the world that would prove the event would happen soon. On 15 June 1911, *The Watchtower* advertised, at sixty times the price of regular wheat, 'Miracle Wheat' that 'should produce ten to fifteen times as much proportionately to the amount sown.' The Department of Agriculture compared it with a regular variety and found the latter was only twice as fruitful! This did not deter Russell who went on to claim other 'miracle' plants such as the 'Millennial Bean' and the 'Wonderful Cotton Seed.' He also advertised cures for cancer and appendicitis.

Russell died on 31 October 1916 on a train at Pampa, Texas, without ever seeing the fulfilment of the return of Christ, whether visible or invisible.

Joseph Franklin Rutherford

The rest of 1916 could be described as the winter of discontent for the WBTS. Bitter in-fighting took place and it was not until 6 January 1917 that Rutherford was elected the second president.

Born 8 November 1869 in Morgan County, Missouri, Rutherford's father was a Baptist but Joseph never liked their 'hell-fire preaching.' In 1894, he bought three volumes of Russell's *Millennial Dawn* and twelve years later in 1906 Rutherford was baptised into the Society.

After the turbulent months before Rutherford's election as president, it was not surprising that on 17 July 1917 opposition erupted when the seventh and final volume of *Millennial Dawn* was released. Opponents claimed that the book merely contained some quotations from Russell's pen, but that Rutherford in this volume repudiated Russell's teachings and substituted newly invented errors. The Society's 1975 Yearbook says 4000 left the Society at this time, which would be approximately 20 per cent of the then membership! Rutherford explained the split as the 'fiery trial' of 1 Pet. 4:12-13. Apparently this was the first, but since often-repeated ploy of finding Scriptures to fit events after they happened. If successful this would 'prove' that the Society is 'God's organisation' foretold by Jehovah in His Word.

Rutherford, like Russell, had problems over his writings and in 1918, with seven others he was convicted of espionage and sent to Atlanta Penitentiary. Again though, Rutherford saw the opportunity to turn this to the Society's advantage when in 1919 with the war over and public opinion easing the offenders were released. The imprisonment was explained as the trampling down of those who look after the 'holy city' (Rev. 11:2-11) and their spiritual killing. Their release is escape from Babylonish captivity. What these explanations fail to add is that many 'Babylonish' clergymen were also in jail for the same reasons.

The Society also claims that in 1919 Jehovah chose the WBTS by delivering the leaders from prison and anointing them with holy spirit to be his remnant to bring in the Kingdom. What is amazing about this, is if Jehovah accepted the WBTS as the only organisation fulfilling His will in 1919, He must now reject it because there have been so many changes and alterations to what it was believing and practising in 1919.

Rutherford continued with Russell's belief that Christ returned invisibly in 1874 but needed to seek out a new date for the return of the Old Testament saints and the setting up of God's Kingdom on earth. In 1920 he published the book *Millions Now Living Will Never Die* which foretold the return to this earth of Abraham, Isaac and Jacob during 1925. 'As we have heretofore stated, the great jubilee cycle is due to begin in 1925.' (*Millions Now Living Will Never Die*, 1925, p. 89)

By 1930 these 'princes', as they were known, had still not returned but a house named *Beth-Sarim* was purchased in San Diego for the resurrected Old Testament saints to live in. (See *Salvation*, 1939, p. 311) The deeds of the house were made out for Rutherford to be allowed to live in the house until Abraham, Isaac or one of the saints came to claim their inheritance. More recent investigation indicates that the rest of the leadership of the WBTS was happy for Rutherford to live in San Diego to keep his drink problem away from the New York headquarters. (See article in Christian Research Journal, Sept-Oct 1997.)

Rutherford had a slogan that 'all religion was a snare and a racket.' If that were shown to be true then there needed to be some clear distinctions between the WBTS and other churches. He therefore made many changes to the 'doctrines' of the Society. We call them changes but *WT*, 15 May 1995, calls them 'Flashes of Light'. Very interestingly, we are told that the Society has received these particularly since 1919. (p. 18)

In 1923, because of the changes in the belief that the Jews no longer would be part of God's plan, the 'other sheep' were brought down to have an earthly inheritance.

1925 was the first time that the organisation proclaimed the importance of the name of Jehovah, although they were not called Jehovah's Witnesses until six years later in 1931.

1927 saw the first resurrection moved to 1918 from 1878. In

addition, this was the same year that the policy on the life being in the blood took shape.

1928 was both the year that Christmas became pagan and should not to be celebrated and the cross should not be used as a symbol any longer. Up until that time the organisation had been involved in both practices. It was a further eight years later, in 1936 that it was determined that Jesus died on a stake and not the cross.

The 'other sheep' were first baptised in 1934 and one year later they were determined to be the same as the 'great multitude.'

1935 saw both a division made between those who could and could not take the bread and the wine and the declaration that Witnesses must not salute the flag.

1939 brought the very timely declaration on neutrality.

Despite this latter declaration, the Society had sought a compromise with Hitler a few years earlier. Dr James Penton, in an article published in *The Christian Quest*, Spring 1990, shows that the so-called 'faithful and discreet slave' tried to make a pact with the Third Reich as a Declaration passed at the 1933 Berlin Convention confirms.

After all these changes Rutherford still made a further date change which was published in the 1941 publication *Children*. In this book, Witnesses were advised to wait until after Armageddon to marry. A copy was given to every child at the summer conventions, and they were told to use it in the 'remaining months before Armageddon.'

Rutherford died of cancer on 8 January 1942 but this time there was no in-fighting for the leadership. This was largely because individualism had been stamped out during Rutherford's time as president. This is probably best illustrated by the change in the 'faithful and discreet slave' from Russell to the organisation.

> Some have claimed that the Scripture, 'the faithful and wise servant', specifically applies to Brother Russell. He never made that claim himself. That Brother Russell was

greatly used of the Lord no one can doubt who knew him. That the Lord used him more wonderfully than anyone on earth since St. Paul's day there can be no doubt. But that does not at all affect the explanation of this scripture. It is clearly manifest from the scriptures hereinbefore cited that the elect Servant of God is Christ, Jesus the Head and his body members; and that Christ Jesus speaks of these faithful members as a part of himself. To say that 'that faithful and wise servant' specifically applies to one individual and to none other would imply that a large proportion of the body members of Christ could not be classed either as faithful or wise. That would be doing violence to the scripture. (*WT*, 15 February 1927, p. 56)

Nathan Homer Knorr

Knorr became the third president of the WBTS on 13 January 1942. He was born 23 April 1905 in Bethlehem, Pennsylvania and was brought up in the Dutch Reformed Church. Baptised into the organisation in 1923 he joined the headquarters staff in Brooklyn New York soon afterwards. Once he became president, he had a self-contained flat with valet and personal kitchen; others had one room, communal bathroom and toilet and mass-produced meals.

He was less conspicuous than his predecessors were. It was said that, 'Russell was fire, Rutherford was acid and ice, and Knorr rock and grey.' He was also described as a 'plodding man' but his forte was organisation and he took the Society from a membership of approximately 108,000 to over 2,000,000.

In 1947, he undertook a world tour on which he arranged for all countries to be more closely tied to Brooklyn. Then in 1950, he arranged for the translation of the Jehovah's Witness Bible, the *New World Translation*. Officially the translator's names have never been released but they are commonly believed to be Frederick Franz, Nathan Knorr, Albert Schroeder and George Gangas.

Probably the major event of his presidency came in 1975 with another failed prophecy! Since 1968 the Society had been encouraging Jehovah's Witnesses to believe that 6000 years of man's existence on earth would end in 1975 and that the thousand-year reign of Christ would begin on earth.

> Why are you looking forward to 1975? What about all this talk concerning the year 1975? Lively discussions, some based on speculation, have burst into flame during recent months among serious students of the Bible. Their interest has been kindled by the belief that 1975 will mark the end of 6,000 years of human history since Adam's creation. The nearness of such an important date indeed fires the imagination and presents unlimited possibilities for discussion. (*WT*, 15 August 1968, p. 494)

Knorr then needed to preside over the early stages of the 'cover-up' even if he did not spearhead it. It was agreed that the Governing Body would blame Witnesses for making 'too much' of a date that the Governing Body only 'intimated was a possibility.'

> With the appearance of the book *Life Everlasting – in Freedom of the Sons of God*, and its comments as to how appropriate it would be for the millennial reign of Christ to parallel the seventh millennium of man's existence, considerable expectation was aroused regarding the year 1975. There were statements made then, and thereafter, stressing that this was only a possibility. UNFORTUNATELY, HOWEVER, ALONG WITH SUCH CAUTIONARY INFORMATION, THERE WERE OTHER STATEMENTS PUBLISHED THAT IMPLIED THAT SUCH A REALIZATION OF HOPES BY THAT YEAR WERE MORE OF A PROBABILITY THAN A MERE POSSIBILITY. It is regretted that these latter statements apparently overshadowed the cautionary ones and contributed to a build-up of the expectation already initiated. (*WT*, 15 March 1980, p. 17)

Many left the organisation as a result of the 1975 failure; some estimate as many as 250,000 in the USA alone.

In 1976, one year before his death, Knorr reluctantly agreed a change in the structure of the Governing Body, and six extra committees were formed. These took much of the traditional authority away from the office of president. Today any change needs a two-thirds majority of all the Governing Body.

Knorr died on 6 May 1977 of a cancerous tumour leaving the way open for Frederick Franz to step into his shoes.

Frederick W. Franz

Born in Covington, Kentucky in 1893, Franz cut short his stay at university to become a full-time preacher for the WBTS. He only took two years Greek at university and was self-taught in Hebrew but he was still regarded as the best Bible translator the Society had! In a Scottish trial in 1954, Frederick Franz was going to have the same sort of problem that Russell had had before him. Under oath he answered questions as follows:

Q. 'Have you also made yourself familiar with Hebrew?'
A. 'Yes.'
Q, 'So that you have a substantial linguistic apparatus at your command?'
A. 'Yes, for use in my biblical work.'
Q. 'You, yourself, read and speak Hebrew, do you?'
A. 'I do not speak Hebrew.'
Q. 'You do not?'
A. 'No.'
Q. 'Can you, yourself, translate that into Hebrew?'
A. 'Which?'
Q. 'The fourth verse of the second chapter of Genesis?'
A. 'You mean here?'
Q. 'Yes?'
A. 'No. I wouldn't attempt to do that.'

(*Purser's Proof*, pp. 6-7,102)

In the 1950 August convention at Yankee Stadium, New York, Franz made a pronouncement that was not greeted with great cheer by all Witnesses, in fact many felt they were cheated. Franz changed the 'princes,' who Rutherford had claimed would return to rule the earth in 1925, from the Old Testament saints to the congregational overseers. He then dramatically said that they were 'now amongst us!'

In 1977 at the age of eighty-three he was elected the Society's fourth president. It was to be three years later in 1980 that he watched over the biggest shake-up at Watchtower headquarters since Rutherford's early days.

As many Witnesses began reading the Bible without Watchtower publications they found the truth and discovered that the Watchtower was not God's organisation giving them food at the proper time. Some left and some were disfellow-shipped, including Franz's own nephew, Raymond, a one-time member of the Governing Body.

Franz died on 22 December 1992.

Milton G. Henschel

Henschel was born in 1920 into a second-generation Witness family living in Pomona, New Jersey. He was baptised into the organisation in 1934 at the age of fourteen. He was secretary to Knorr when he made his world trip in 1945.

In 1968 he proclaimed that transplanting organs is really cannibalism (interview with *Detroit Free Press*) and in the same interview that 1975 was a year to watch.

He was elected as the fifth president of the WBTS on 30 December 1992. With the rest of the Governing Body, he is pre-siding over shaky times with numbers in Europe dropping and the challenge to the policy on blood.

3

The Organisation and it's Practices

___ ை ___

Propoganda

If we are going to reach the Jehovah's Witnesses for Christ, we must understand them. Why do they react like they do? Why are they so difficult to talk to? Why don't they see the argument you are putting forward?

It all comes down to mind control. From day one, the Witness is only given limited and specially prepared information that puts the organisation in a favourable light. At the same time, they are fed information that every other group is wrong. This controls them into the Watchtower way of thinking. When you add to this the lengths to which the Society will go to cut them off from close family and any other friends and relatives who might affect their thinking you will see that the new Jehovah's Witness becomes an island in the midst of the sea of Watchtower propaganda.

Material Jehovah's Witnesses must not read

> Consider some of the other 'twisted things' used to mislead God's people today. On occasion opposers will question the various teachings that Jehovah's people hold in common ... They may question the need for an organization to direct the minds of God's people. Their view is, God's spirit can direct individuals without some central, organized body of men giving direction. They will declare that all one needs to do is read the Bible. But Christendom has been reading the Bible for centuries.

31

And look at the indistinct trumpet call coming from Christendom today!... What a contrast this is to the foretold peace and unity among true Christians who not only read the Bible but search out and zealously apply its teachings (Eph 4:3-6) ... What then is our position toward those who oppose and seek to undermine the faith we have received through Jehovah's Witnesses and the Christian 'organization' Jehovah is using? ... To quarrel with such ones, to debate and argue, is futile and really not the Christian course. (*WT*, 1 March 1983, p. 25) (See also *WT*, 15 March 1986, pp. 13-14)

God deals with an organisation, not individuals.

Jehovah God deals with his people as a servant class. He does not feed each one individually nor does he appoint an individual over them. No individual student of God's Word reveals God's will or interprets his Word (2 Pet 1:20,21). God interprets and teaches, through Christ the Chief Servant, who in turn uses the discreet slave as the visible channel, the visible theocratic organization ... We should eat and assimilate what is set before us, without shying away from parts of the food because it may not suit the fancy of our mental taste. The truths we are to publish are the ones provided through the discreet slave organization, not some personal opinions contrary to what the slave has provided as timely food. Jehovah and Christ direct and correct the slave as needed, not we as individuals ... We should meekly go along with the Lord's theocratic organization, rather than balk at the first mention of a thought unpalatable to us and proceed to quibble and mouth our criticisms and opinions as though they were worth more than the slave's provision of spiritual food. Theocratic ones will appreciate the Lord's visible organization and not be so foolish as to pit against Jehovah's channel their own human reasoning and sentiment and personal feelings. (*WT*, 1 February 1952, pp. 79-80)

The Bible cannot shine forth life-giving truth by itself.

Jehovah God has provided his holy written Word for all mankind ... But God has not arranged for that Word to speak independently ... It is through his organization that God, provides this light that the proverb says is the teaching or law of the mother. If we are to walk in the light of truth we must recognize not only Jehovah God as our Father but his organization as our mother. (*WT*, 1 May 1957, p. 274)

Individuals cannot interpret the Bible.

Thus the Bible is an organizational book and belongs to the Christian congregation as an organization, not to individuals, regardless of how sincerely they may believe that they can interpret the Bible. For this reason the Bible cannot be properly understood without Jehovah's visible organization in mind. (*WT*, 1 October 1967, p. 587)

Only God's Holy Spirit directs this organisation.

Consider, too, the fact that Jehovah's organization alone, in all the earth, is directed by God's holy spirit or active force (Zech. 4:6). Only this organization functions for Jehovah's purpose and to his praise. To it alone God's Sacred Word, the Bible, is not a sealed book. (*WT*, 1 July 1973, p. 402)

The organisation must be permitted to think for you.

Fight Against Independent Thinking ... Yet there are some who point out that the organization has had to make some adjustments before, and so they argue: 'This shows that we have to make up our own mind on what to believe.' This is independent thinking. Why is it so dangerous? Such thinking is an evidence of pride ... If we get to thinking that we know better than the organization, we should ask ourselves: 'Where did we learn Bible truth in the first place? Would we know the way of the truth if it had not been for guidance from the organization? Really, can we get along without the direction of God's organization?' No we cannot! (*WT*, 15 January 1983, p. 27)

The 'book of knowledge'

It all begins so innocently when the Witness will invite the householder to undertake a 'Bible Study'. This will turn out to be a book study, which at present will be the book *Knowledge That Leads to Everlasting Life*. The Witness will read the first couple of paragraphs and will ask a question printed at the bottom of the page. This question is numbered to correspond with the paragraph numbers just read. In the current book this will be, 'What does your Creator want for you?' The answer derived from the passage will be, 'lasting happiness under the best conditions in wonderful surroundings.' You will also discover that God has given the key to this happy future and, 'that key is knowledge.'

What you do not realise at the time is that the paragraph has been written by the WBTS. The question has then been asked by the WBTS to get you to answer according to the information given to you by the WBTS. This is the subtle way that the Jehovah's Witnesses begin to change your belief system and control what you think. However, the way they begin is the way they intend to carry on and most of the five one-hour gatherings each week follow a similar pattern.

The Home Group Study

This is a logical step, because here a Society's publication is studied in the same manner as in your home. Each paragraph of the publication is numbered, and an appropriately numbered question is printed at the bottom of the page. The paragraph is first read, and then the study conductor asks the question that relates to the paragraph and in which the answer can be found. The group normally consists of about fifteen to twenty Witnesses.

The Kingdom Hall
Most Kingdom Halls, the WBTS's name for its meeting places, are purpose-built, modern, single-storey buildings. Often you will find one going up in your area over a weekend. The Society is well prepared and organised to accomplish these 'quick builds'.

Sunday meetings consist of two one-hour back-to-back meetings. First,

The Public Talk
This is the only regular meeting that does not have audience participation. After a song and a brief prayer, a responsible brother in the organisation gives a talk lasting about forty-five minutes on a subject and outline set by the Society. When it is over they sing another song and go straight into the ...

Watchtower Study
Every edition of The Watchtower magazine contains two main articles, which follow the same pattern as the home book study – numbered paragraphs with appropriate questions at the bottom of the page. The Watchtower Overseer takes this part of the meeting, which normally lasts between 45 and 55 minutes. On the platform with the overseer is a male Witness who is ready to read the appropriate paragraph. After a welcome the overseer will announce which article they are studying and ask the first question. He will then ask the other Witness to read the paragraphs and then repeats the question and looks up for any with raised hands.

As someone is selected to give the answer, a brother takes a roving microphone to him or her. When the question has been answered to the satisfaction of the Watchtower Overseer, he reads the next question, has the paragraph read, and the process starts all over again, until the whole article has been thoroughly studied.

The other two regular meetings are usually held back-to-back on a Thursday night at the Kingdom Hall.

The Ministry School

All Jehovah's Witnesses are normally enrolled in the Ministry School. The women give demonstrations; one will play the part of a Witness and the other a householder with a 'worldly' or 'Biblical' problem. In this school, the Witnesses are trained to prove that the Society is right in all its teachings.

The men give short talks which are 'marked' by the Ministry School Overseer on a thirty-six-point counsel sheet. The student works through each of the thirty-six points, receiving the mark: G-good; I-improved; or W-work on it. Once each of the thirty-six points has been covered the student starts all over again. Some of the wide variety of points they are marked on include: informative material; volume; Scriptural application; gestures; illustrations; timing; being clear and understandable; pausing; repetition; emphasis of subject theme; conversational quality; and personal appearance.

Each week five students take part, and sometimes a second ministry school is held in an adjoining room in the Kingdom Hall. In this way, each student gets between two and four assignments each year. The Ministry School lasts around forty-five minutes and is followed by:

The Service Meeting

The Service Meeting discusses an internal paper that today is called *Our Kingdom Ministry*. It contains the weekly programme for the meetings, talks, study articles, demonstrations, and discussions. Everything is designed to stimulate more and more effort from the Witnesses. Some encouragements from recent editions include:

Can you serve where there is greater need? (November 1997)

Speak about Jehovah every day (December 1997)

Our absence from a weekly meeting can affect the spiritual well-being of others who attend. If you are not there, be assured – you are missed! (December 1997)

Jesus Christ put the responsibility to evangelize on all his disciples... may we be motivated to share the exciting Kingdom good news... (February 1998)

What are your plans for the summer? ... Summertime affords us a variety of opportunities to advance theocratic interests ... Why not plan to increase your field activity ... plan ahead to auxiliary pioneer in August, when there will be five full weekends ... If you will be vacationing away from home, plan to attend the meetings and share in the field service with the congregation in the locality ... energize yourself spiritually by continuing to put the Kingdom first in your life. (May 1998)

At this meeting, a capable Witness demonstrates the ideal sermon of the month, to be used on the doors.

Indoctrination Programme

As the majority of these meetings need some form of congregation participation, personal study is vital. Surely, this would show up any false Biblical doctrines the Society was teaching. Here another part of mind control takes place. Witnesses do not have time to fully research what they are reading, so they take on trust what they are being taught. It is easy to see how the Society is able to manipulate its followers into wrong views. It is no surprise, then, to find the following instruction:

> We may think of study as hard work, as involving heavy research. But in Jehovah's organization IT IS NOT NECESSARY TO SPEND A LOT OF TIME AND ENERGY IN RESEARCH, for there are brothers in the organization who are assigned to do that

very thing, to help you who do not have so much time for this, these preparing the good material in *The Watchtower* and other publications of the Society. (*WT*, 1 June 1967, p. 338)

What Jehovah's Witnesses think of as study is not deep research, but is simply reading the assigned Watchtower material, then the Watchtower questions at the bottom of the page, and underlining the Watchtower answers within the cited paragraphs.

The following Watchtower statements underline this attitude:

1. The Watchtower Society is God's sole visible channel. (*WT*, 1 October 1967, p. 590)
2. You must come into the Society for salvation. (*WT*, 15 November 1981, p. 21)
3. Therefore they know better than you. (*WT*, 1 February 1952, p. 80)
4. Avoid thinking for yourself, which is really an evidence of pride. (*WT*, 15 January 1983, p. 27)

Many Witnesses are caught with nowhere to look for guidance outside the organisation. The zealousness, the genuineness, the very organised methods, and the apparent lack of these things in the churches, combine to convince them that it is the direction of God that is causing the WBTS to march ever onward. They have not recognised the mind-control techniques that they have been subjected to, and now, even if they were pointed out to them, they would not understand. Probably they would believe that it was Satan trying to get them to leave Jehovah's organisation.

The Structure of the Organisation
The organisational structure of the Watchtower Society is the key to its total control. A small select group called the

Governing Body directs the Society and its followers from the headquarters in Brooklyn, New York, USA. In turn, a Branch Committee which answers back to the Governing Body supervises each country.

Each Branch divides up the country into smaller Districts. Each District is subdivided into Circuits comprising fifteen or so congregations. Circuit Overseers are appointed to supervise and serve the needs of the congregations in a particular Circuit. In turn, District Overseers are appointed to oversee a number of Circuits, visiting them and speaking at their Circuit assemblies. Normally there are three Circuit assemblies and one District assembly each year. At the District assembly, several Circuits meet together in huge stadiums or halls. The Circuit assembly is held during a Saturday and Sunday, and a District assembly will be three or more days.

In each local congregation, there is a Presiding Overseer; a Secretary (a male witness); a Service Overseer; a Watchtower Study Overseer; and a Ministry School Overseer. Those who really run the congregation are known as the Congregation Service Committee, comprising the Presiding Overseer, Secretary and Service Overseer. These are responsible for any disciplinary measures that are taken. The Society prefers local home groups to be run by elders. Beneath the elders come the ministerial servants, a number of men who take charge of the more mundane matters in the congregation.

The ordinary Jehovah's Witness is known as a 'publisher,' because he publishes Watchtower teachings from door to door. The publisher is expected to devote ten hours each month to this door-to-door activity. Certain members within the congregations arrange their affairs to spend more time in the door-to-door work, the hours they are asked to spend changed early in 1999. These are known as:

Auxiliary pioneers – 50 hours monthly.
Regular pioneers – 70 hours monthly.
Special pioneers – approximately 140 hours monthly.

Of these, only the 'special pioneers' receive small financial assistance, but all have to do part-time work to pay their way.

'God's Organisation'

The modern-day Jehovah's Witness believes that the WBTS alone is God's organisation and that its leaders, the Governing Body are only answerable to Jehovah God. These men are the only mouthpiece for Jehovah on this earth. The structure of the Society underneath the Governing Body, with its assisting committees, is a pyramid structure.

Later we will see the difference between the leaders, the 'faithful and discreet slave' class or 'little flock' and 'the other sheep'. For now it is enough for us to know that there is a difference and that originally only the elite group of the 'little flock' could be seen to be leading the Society. However, these men are getting older and so changes have been made in recent years.

The *WT*, 15 April, 1992 announced on p. 31 that because the remnant of the anointed is decreasing and the great crowd increasing alterations needed to take place.

> In view of the tremendous increase world-wide, it seems appropriate at this time to provide the Governing Body with some additional assistance. Therefore it has been decided to invite several helpers, mainly from among the great crowd, to share in the meetings of each of the Governing Body Committees ... Thus, the number attending the meetings of each of these committees will be increased to seven or eight. Under the direction of the Governing Body committee members, these assistants will take part in discussions and will carry out various assignments given them by the committee. This new arrangement goes into effect May 1,1992.

So much emphasis is placed upon 'God's organisation' that a Witness finds it very difficult to question or entertain doubts about its validity. Indeed, although they may never admit it, the organisation becomes almost as important as Jehovah and certainly more important than Jesus.

The Society's 'proof' regarding the organisation is that there was only one organisation in the early church and therefore there is only one organisation today. But is the basis of membership of this organisation an inward spiritual relationship? No. 'Members of an organization are united by administrative arrangements and by standards or requirements.' – *Reasoning*, p. 280

Reasoning, pp. 283/284 then lists seven identifying marks of Jehovah's visible organisation. Summarised, these are:

1. Exalt Jehovah as the true God.
2. Recognise Jesus' vital role in Jehovah's purpose.
3. Adhere closely to God's Word.
4. Keep separate from the world.
5. Maintain a high level of moral cleanliness.
6. Preach the good news.
7. Cultivate fruits of the spirit.

The article does not conclude by saying the WBTS is the one but it certainly infers it. However, we would argue that the Society falls down on some of those points whereas other churches do not. Nevertheless, in the end we need to check, with the Scriptures, its claim that there is only one organisation today.

An article entitled, 'Direct New Ones to God's Organization' found in *WT*, 1 November 1984, makes several statements that we can check.

According to this article, Paul and other Christians did not make their own decisions on doctrinal matters but received 'authoritative answers' from the elders in Jerusalem. However, we read in another article:

Was the apostle Paul part of the Christian governing body? It is reasonable to conclude that Paul was a part of the Christian governing body in the first century. (*WT*, 1 December 1985, p. 31)

The first article tells us that Paul went to Jerusalem to 'explain' the good news he was preaching. However, if as the second article states, Paul was part of the governing body, surely it would know! But did Paul go to Jerusalem to check if he was 'running in vain'?

Why did Paul go to Jerusalem?
A careful look at Gal. 2 shows what happened.

- Paul went to those of reputation in Jerusalem because of the revelation given to him by the Lord. (Gal. 2:1-2)
- The men of reputation in Jerusalem contributed nothing to Paul which is a very strange way of giving an authoritative answer! (Gal. 2:6)
- The elders simply made a request to Paul and Barnabas that they should remember the poor. (Gal. 2:10)
- Later, Paul had to oppose Peter, one of the elders from Jerusalem, because he was not living the Christian life in a full and open way. (Gal. 2:11-14)

It is evident that the Watchtower's interpretation of these events is wrong. There was not one organisation in the New Testament church and so there is no ground for one organisation today. If a Witness still does not want to accept the truth of Scripture share this thought. The first 'Governing Body' was allowing false doctrine to be preached until someone came in from the outside to correct them! Is it the same today?

What it means to be a 'Witness'
Once the individual is convinced that this is the only organisation God is using today, they will be willing to work for it.

Apart from the study and meetings that we have already looked at, what will that entail?

Baptism

On average for the first six to nine months the new Witness will be working towards being baptised. They will study various questions on the organisation in a Watchtower book. The one still used at the time of writing is called *Organized to Accomplish Our Ministry* (1983 publication).

Starting on page 175 are the 'Questions for those desiring to be baptised.' In order to be accepted for baptism the Witness must answer to the satisfaction of one of the local elders, these approximately 125 questions.

On page 173 we read:

> The information that follows in this section will serve as a review to help you examine yourself regarding your understanding of Jehovah's purposes and the opportunities set before you to serve him. The questions provide the basis for the congregation elders to have some helpful discussions with you. In reviewing these questions with you, the elders will help you determine whether you have become qualified to be baptised in water as a symbol of your dedication to God.

Normally baptisms take place at a larger gathering of several congregations, a circuit assembly or annual convention. The baptismal candidates will be seated in the front rows and listen to a half-hour talk. At the conclusion of the talk, they will be asked to stand and answer in the affirmative two questions:

> 1. On the basis of the sacrifice of Jesus Christ, have you repented of your sins and dedicated yourself to Jehovah to do his will?
> 2. Do you understand that your dedication and baptism identify you as one of Jehovah's Witnesses in association

with God's spirit-directed 'organization'. (*WT*, 1 June 1985, p. 30)

After answering in the affirmative, the candidates are baptised in front of the assembled congregations, by total immersion. No personal testimonies are given, and no baptismal formula is said over them as they are baptised.

Door-to-door work

The Society will impress on all its members that they should 'preach this good news of the kingdom' to others, because someone came to them in the first place. Soon after joining the congregation, they will be encouraged to get out on the doors.

Normally, the Witness first taking the new member out will endeavour to call on interested persons, possibly even get them to help with home book studies they are conducting. The new recruit will have been warned that Satan opposes the preaching of this 'good news' and therefore, at some time in the work, opposition is bound to confront them. They will meet with people who will try to discourage them and the preaching. Taking all this on board and dedicating themselves to serving Jehovah they will begin to find the ten hours a month suggested as a minimum that should be spent on the doors.

Doctrine and Beliefs Chart

The table on page 45 is an overview of Watchtower beliefs on central doctrines and compares it with mainline Christian doctrine. Only doctrines of significant difference are listed. Where further explanation is needed, for example regarding John 1:1, this will be found in the following chapters.

Subject	Jehovah's Witness	Christian	Scripture
Bible	We agree in words that the Bible is the inspired Word of God but in reality the WBTS has changed it many times. See appropriate chapters.		
God	1. Only Jehovah is God 2. Must use His personal name	1. The Father is one member of the Godhead 2. Personal name not recorded in New Testament	Deut. 6:4 Acts 4:10-12
Jesus	1. Jesus is a created being 2. Same as the Archangel Michael 3. Jesus is 'a god' but not Almighty God	1. Jesus is eternal 2. Jesus cannot be an angel 3. Jesus is God	Heb. 7:3 Heb. 1:7,8 John 1:1
Holy Spirit	1. Not a person, nor God. Likened to an electric force	1. Is a part of the Godhead 2. Has the attributes of a person	Acts 5:3,4 1 Cor. 12:11
Trinity	1. A pagan doctrine	1. Revealed in Scripture	Matt. 28:19
Salvation	1. Two-tier salvation - 144,000 in heaven, great crowd on earth 2. Salvation is a reward not a gift	1. Salvation is the same basis for everyone All the redeemed in the same place 2. Salvation is a gift	Rev. 21:1-3 Eph. 2:8-10
Cross	1. Jesus did not die on a cross but on a stake. 2. Hands above His head therefore only one nail	1. Jesus was crucified in the manner of the Romans 2. Arms outstretched, therefore two nails	Matt. 27:22,26,31-33 John 20:25
Spirit and Soul	1. No eternal spirit in man - simply goes back to dust	1. Eternal spirit that goes back to God at death.	1 Thess. 5:10 Heb. 12:23
Death and Hell	1. Death is simply the opposite of life 2. Hell is the common grave	1. Death is also used as spiritual death 2. Hell is place of eternal destruction away from God	Matt. 10:28 Matt. 25:46; Mark 9:43
Resurrection	1. Involves reactivating life pattern. Keeps the same identity as had when died. 2. Can be a human or a spirit body 3. Some will be annihilated and not have a resurrection at all 4. Jesus was resurrected as a spirit person.	1. Will have a resurrection body and be new creatures 2. All have the same resurrection 3. Everyone has a form of eternal life - no annihilation 4. Jesus had a glorified resurrection body.	1 Cor. 15:42-44 Rev. 20:11-15 1 Cor. 15:12-13 Luke 24:39
Special Days	It is against Jehovah and His word to celebrate birthdays, Christmas, Easter, etc.	Celebration is a matter of conscience and glorifying God	Col. 2:16-17
Blood	God forbids us to take blood transfusions	Nowhere is blood transfusion dealt with in Scripture. This is a matter of conscience.	

1999 Statistics

The figures as published at the beginning of 1999 are:

	World-wide	Britain
Peak publishers:	5,888,650	131,981
New Witnesses baptised:	316,092	3,375
Hours on the doors:	1,186,666,708	20,088,395
Memorial meal attendance:	13,896,312	214,351
Memorial meal partakers:	8,756	

From 1996 to 1998 the number of Jehovah's Witnesses in Britain has fallen from 124,623 to 123,191. World-wide the average increase in this period is 3.8% but Europe overall is falling in numbers whereas areas such as Albania, Bangladesh, Belarus and Bosnia & Herzegovina bring hefty increases.

The breakdown for some European countries with a negative growth rate in 1998 is

Austria -1%	Liechtenstein -6%
Belgium -1%	Netherlands -1%
Denmark -1%	Spain -1%
France -2%	Sweden -1%
Germany 0%	Switzerland -1%.

Italy however, goes against the trend with +2%. The conclusion is obvious though; developing countries are welcoming the Watchtower with open arms whereas many of the countries that it has been in for years are rejecting Jehovah's Witnesses.

4

The Godhead – Father

The Watchtower belief is that Jehovah alone is God. Christians have no problem with the fact that Jehovah, the Father, is God, but it is when the word 'alone' is put in that the problems start.

Another area of difference is the way a Witness will look at the Father. To many, He is a hard taskmaster who after forty years dedication could annihilate you at Armageddon because you smoked. Most Witnesses would not verbalise their belief like this but those are the facts when all the 'packing' is taken away. It might be true that some Christians rely too much on grace and forget the commandments of God but for the Witness it is the other way round. You can helpfully share with them the evidence for the loving heart of the Father as in Luke 15 with His prodigal son.

One other difference is in the character of God – He is not omnipresent – one of the characteristics that makes God, God.

> ... (1 Kings 8:27) ... Solomon's statement does not mean that God has no specific place of residence. Nor does it mean that he is omnipresent in the sense of BEING LITERALLY EVERYWHERE and in everything. (*Insight*, Vol. 1, p. 1060)

If by this is meant that He is not in everything in the pantheistic sense, we would agree, but the Bible says that He is everywhere!

The Watchtower also says that He is not part of a trinity. We will deal with whether Jesus and the Holy Spirit make up the Trinity under those sections but here we want to look at the claim by the WBTS that we must use the name of Jehovah if we want to be Christians.

The name of Jehovah

'Every lover of righteousness who reads the inspired Scriptures and who truly comes to 'know' with understanding the full meaning of Jehovah's name ... has every reason therefore, to love and bless that name ...' (*Insight*, Vol. 2, p. 20)

According to the Witness we must use this name. If we do not then we do not love Jehovah as we should and are not truly serving the living God. This subject will arise eventually and so we need to understand what a Witness believes and have some idea of how to answer.

The case it makes revolves around four Hebrew consonants (YHWH) found in Old Testament manuscripts. These letters are known as the tetragrammaton (abbreviated to tetragram) and today commonly recognised as 'Jehovah'. The Society acknowledges the fact that this is not the best pronunciation.

Hebrew scholars generally favor 'Yahweh' as the most likely pronunciation ... Since certainty of pronunciation is not now attainable, there seems no reason for abandoning in English the well-known form 'Jehovah' in favor of some other suggested pronunciation. (*Insight*, Vol. 2, p. 7)

However, leaving aside what seems to be the secondary issue of pronunciation we need to look at three central claims made by the WBTS regarding the use of 'Jehovah' in the New Testament and the early church. If these claims are right then we should be using 'Jehovah' today but if wrong, the very basis on which the Society stands is faulty.

The Society claims in *Insight*, Vol. 2, pp. 5-20; *NWT*, with references, 1984, pp. 1561-66; and *KIT*, pp. 10-15 that,

1. The tetragram is found in the early Greek translation of the Old Testament, known as the Septuagint (abbreviated to LXX).
2. Jesus and His followers in the early church would pronounce the tetragram every time they came across it.
3. The tetragram was originally to be found in the Greek manuscripts of the New Testament but sometime during the second or third centuries, copyists who did not appreciate, or developed an aversion for, the divine name removed it.

Claim 1: the tetragram is found instead of a Greek word in the LXX

This is truth, but not the whole truth, and in any case, here the Society contradicts itself. It bases its case almost entirely on the discovery of a part copy of the LXX called 'P. Fouad Inv. No. 266'. Dated first or second century BC, it contains parts of Deut. 18:5-32:19. (See *Insight*, Vol. 1, p. 326) This is almost certainly of Jewish origin because it is written in square Hebrew characters on a scroll. The Society concludes that because this one copy of the LXX contains the tetragram then all copies must have, especially the ones that Jesus read. Nevertheless, in an earlier publication we read '"Jehovah" does not occur in the Septuagint version, that name being represented by the Greek words for "the Lord".' (*Equipped for Every Good Work*, WBTS, 1946, p. 53)

What makes this contradiction even more remarkable is that the Deuteronomy fragments were first published in 1944 and the *Equipped* book was not published until 1946.

There were many versions of the LXX and some used by the Jews would have had the four Hebrew letters but most did not have any special wording at all. Most, if not all, of the versions that the Society quote are of Jewish origin and therefore the scribes, translating or copying, would be simply keeping to their traditions by using the tetragram. We should also note that the Society has carefully avoided mention of another portion of the LXX called 'P. Ryl. GK. 458', dated middle second century BC. C. H. Roberts points out in *Two Biblical Papyri*, p. 44, 'it is probable that *kyrios* was written in full.' In other words, this version probably did not contain the tetragram.

For additional study on this see p. 203.

Claim 2: Jesus and His followers pronounced the divine name, and therefore we should today

As already shown, only two BC copies of the LXX have been brought forward for evidence. Therefore, it is a wild assumption to say that the manuscript Jesus read in the synagogue contained the tetragram. However, just for a minute let us accept that this was the case. Would the Scribes and the Pharisees allow Him to pronounce the name without a violent outburst? Luke 4:22 tells us they all began to give favourable witness. I do not believe that this calm, appreciative reaction followed the first time the tetragram had been pronounced in a synagogue for hundreds of years! The reaction only comes later when the Jewish leaders realise He is talking about God choosing Gentiles before Jews.

In addition, if the purpose of Jesus' ministry was to make known the name of God by pronouncing it, He failed. The *NWT* takes pains to show that Jesus used the divine name. However, apart from a dozen or so quotes from the Old Testament (we will look at the validity of these later) it can only find evidence to put 'Jehovah' in the mouth of Jesus twice! Jesus did not make the divine name known by pronouncing it. We close this section with the comments of two biblical scholars about 'Jehovah' in connection with Jesus. It is worth noting that the first, Steve Byington, has translated a modern version of the Bible that the Society promotes.

> If we need to argue the point of translating 'the Lord' where the Greek says 'the Lord', my argument would be

that when Jesus and the apostles and their friends spoke an Old Testament text aloud, they said 'the Lord' for 'Jehovah' even in so careful a quotation as Mark 12:29 (the newly found manuscript of Isaiah may be cited as fresh evidence that the custom of saying 'the Lord' began before the time of Christ ...), and we cannot presume that the apostles wrote otherwise than they spoke. (S. T. Byington, *The Christian Century*, 9 May 1951, p. 589)

Referring initially to the tetragram in the Aquila Fragments, H. H. Rowley wrote in the Expository Times soon after Vol. 2 of the NWT Old Testament was released in 1955:

Actually this offers no evidence that it was pronounced by the reader, any more than it was pronounced by the Jew who read from the Hebrew, where also it was written ... if our Lord had rejected the unwillingness to pronounce the Name ... it might have been expected that His disciples would have noticed and followed Him in this. Such evidence as we have indicates that when He quoted Psalm 110 He used words which mean 'The Lord said unto my Lord,' and not 'Yahweh said unto my Lord.' Similarly, there is no evidence that in Romans 9:29,15:9, or 2 Corinthians 6:17 Paul ever wrote anything other than *kyrios* to represent the (tetragram).

Claim 3: the tetragram appears in the original New Testament manuscripts

This is the WBTS's equivalent of the theory of evolution. There is no evidence but it must be. In fact, all the evidence points in the other direction. There is not one New Testament manuscript known today in which the tetragram appears and there is no evidence of a conspiracy to get rid of the tetragram.

The Watchtower places its 'burden of proof' on a work by George Howard, published in the *Journal of Biblical Literature*, 1977. The *KIT* (pp. 1137-38), quotes from his work 'In the fol-

lowing pages we will set forth A THEORY that the divine name ...
was originally written in the N[ew] T[estament] quotations of
and allusions to the O[ld] T[estament].'

As we have emphasised, this is a theory, and Professor
Howard maintains to this day that it should be treated as a theory until a New Testament manuscript is found with the tetragram. Howard starts his article, 'In order to support this theory,'
and ends:

> Concluding observations ... We have refrained from
> drawing too many conclusions due to the revolutionary
> nature of THIS THEORY. Rather than state conclusions now
> in a positive manner it seems better only to raise some
> questions that suggest a need for further examination a)
> IF the tetragram was used in the NT, how extensively was
> it used ...?

Professor Howard clearly then saw the need for caution and further investigation. He still says that until a manuscript of the
New Testament is found with the tetragram his theory remains
a theory. However, the WBTS is not content with that so it concludes the *KIT* article with a quantum leap: 'We concur with
the above, with one exception: We do not consider this view a
'theory', but, rather, a presentation of the FACTS (???) of history
as to the transmission of Bible manuscripts.'

Please note our '???' What facts? Actually, the Society is up
to its normal tricks in missing out much of Howard's article.
One of the relevant parts is: 'We can imagine that the NT text
incorporated the tetragram into its OT quotations and that the
words *kyrios* and *theos* were used when secondary references to
God were made in the comments that were based upon the
quotations.'

Also the article dealt, 'primarily with the divine name as it
was written ... not with what word or words the reader pronounced.'

So even if the WBTS wishes to consider this theory a fact, all it can claim from it is that the divine name would be in the New Testament Scriptures only where it quoted Old Testament Scripture. It has, however, gone far beyond that, even to claiming the pronouncing of the name which Howard says he does not deal with.

For additional study on this see p. 208.

Conclusion from Scriptures

The above shows that the Society's scholarship cannot be trusted but we now need to make some conclusions based on Scripture.

We have seen that the Old Testament revelation included the tetragram but the New Testament does not; so what revelation do we receive of God in the New Testament? Over a hundred times in the Gospels alone we read 'Father'. We see in John 17:6,26 Jesus claimed that He had made the name known. However, we have already shown that Jesus did not pronounce the tetragram so what was He talking about? The Society gives us the answer.

> For an individual to know God's name signifies MORE THAN A MERE ACQUAINTANCE WITH THE WORD ... It means actually knowing the Person ... This is illustrated in the case of Moses ... (he) was privileged ... to 'hear the name of Jehovah declared'. That declaration was NOT SIMPLY THE REPETITION OF THE NAME 'JEHOVAH' ... When Jesus Christ was on earth, he 'made his Father's name manifest' to his disciples (John 17:6,26). Although having earlier known that name and being familiar with God's activities as recorded in the Hebrew Scriptures, these disciples came to know Jehovah in a far better and grander Way ... CHRIST JESUS PERFECTLY REPRESENTED HIS FATHER, doing the works of his Father and speaking, not on his own originality, but the words of his Father. (*Insight*, Vol. 2, pp. 466-7)

In other words, it wasn't so much what Jesus said but what He did that made the name known. Repeatedly Jesus said He did the will of His Father, spoke the words of His Father, did what He saw His Father doing. Not Jehovah but Father. This is the New Testament record. There is no removal of the name-it was never there. If Jesus was who the Society says He was then He should have used 'Jehovah' hundreds of times but He never did.

The Old Testament revelation was Jehovah; the New Testament is Jesus. The Old Testament was outward obedience to Jehovah in sacrifices; the New Testament is knowing Jesus in the heart. The Old Testament saints were to be witnesses of Jehovah; the New Testament ones are to be witnesses of Jesus. We today are privileged to be in the New Testament and we need to live in the glorious free family relationship given to us.

5

The Godhead – Jesus

— ❧ —

Who is Jesus?

The Watchtower belief of who Jesus is can be seen in the Watchtower publication, *The Greatest Man Who Ever Lived*, 1991, and it is different from the Jesus in the Bible. We quote three passages:

> But more than that happens as Jesus is baptized. 'The heavens are opened up' to him. What does this mean? Evidently it means that while he is being baptized, the memory of his pre-human life in heaven returns to him. Thus, Jesus now fully recalls his life as a spirit son of Jehovah God, including all the things that God spoke to him in heaven during his pre-human existence. (Section 12, page 2)

> However at his baptism, Jesus enters into a new relationship with God, becoming also God's spiritual Son. (Section 12, page 3)

> 'Unless anyone is born from water and spirit,' Jesus explains, 'he cannot enter the kingdom of God.' When Jesus was baptized and holy spirit descended upon him, he was thus born 'from water and spirit' ... Later, at Pentecost 33 CE, other baptized ones will receive holy spirit and will thus also be born again as spiritual sons of God. (Section 17, page 2)

Here we discover the following about the Watchtower Jesus:

1. He is only a spirit Son of God.
2. He only became God's spiritual Son at baptism
3. He needed to be born again to see God's kingdom.

A Jehovah's Witness believes that the Jesus described above is the one portrayed in the Bible. We will check this out to see if it is true.

Is Jesus a created being?

The Watchtower will say that Jesus is just a spiritual son because Jehovah created Him. A Scripture the Witness will often turn to in this regard is Rev. 3:14. In the *NWT* this clearly says that Jesus is 'the beginning of the creation by God,' which seems to confirm the Watchtower belief that Jesus is the first one to be created by Jehovah. But does this verse say that?

A look at the *KIT* shows that the Greek is 'of God' not 'by God'. This puts a different light on this verse. The *KIT* also shows us that the Greek word translated 'beginning' is *arche*. In some versions of the Bible, this word is translated 'source' or 'origin', which one is right? Think of the English word 'architect' and you see that they are all right; it means beginning in the sense of source. The architect is the source and designer of the whole building.

Put these two things together and we see that Rev. 3:14 actually says that Jesus is the SOURCE OF ALL GOD'S CREATION, not the first one to be created.

> *Arche* means a beginning. The root *arch-* primarily indicated what was of worth. Hence the verb *archo* meant 'to be first' and *archon* denoted a ruler. So also the idea of a beginning, the origin, the active cause, whether a person or thing. (*Vine*, Vol. 1, p. 111)

The Witnesses also make much of the phrase 'firstborn' and re-translate it in their minds to read, 'the first to be created.'

In Col. 1:15, the Greek word translated 'firstborn' is *proto-tokos* whereas the Greek for 'first-created' would be *protoktistos*. *Prototokos* means the first-begotten and can never mean the first one to be born. Its meaning is priority to or pre-eminence over; therefore Jesus is the pre-eminent one over all creation and not a created being Himself.

Whichever English word is used we must discover what the Greek means. For instance, does Col. 1:18 mean that Jesus was the first one to be born from the dead? That would not be true because Lazarus rose from the dead before him, as indeed did others in the Old and New Testaments. Is the Scripture wrong? No, because the Greek word has the meaning of position, place, or ranking. This is seen in the Old Testament, where on two occasions the first to be born lost the position of firstborn to the second to be born.

Firstborn has always, in the Hebrew tradition, had to do with place and pre-eminence over. The context of Colossians makes it clear that the word is used in the same way. That 'He might come to have first place in everything'. (v. 18)

Is Jesus an angel?

The Watchtower teaches that Jesus, the first creation of Jehovah, is also a special spirit creature, called Michael the Archangel in Scripture. But does the Bible show that Jesus and Michael are the same person?

Dan. 10:13 says that Michael is one of the princes. When we compare Dan. 8:25 we find that Jesus is THE Prince. We see here, and in many other places in Scripture, that Jesus is unique, and yet Michael is not. How can they be the same person?

In Jude 9 Michael says, 'the Lord rebuke you.' However, when Jesus was on this earth He rebuked Satan and the demons directly and they fled before Him. How can this be the same person?

Heb. 1:7 & 8 shows beyond doubt that Jesus is not an angel.

Verse 7 has Jehovah speaking, 'to the angels' The 'but' at the beginning of verse 8 shows us He is talking to someone different, here it is 'to the Son'. The angels are on one side and the Son is on the other and there is a dividing line down the middle. The Son, Jesus, cannot be an angel, not even an archangel because he would still be by nature an angel.

What was declared at Jesus' birth?

The Watchtower teaches that at baptism Jesus enters into a new relationship with Jehovah. Yet, the Scripture says ' . . . for today in the city of David there has been born for you a Saviour, who is Christ the Lord.' (Luke 2:11) Not in thirty years time but 'today'. Not 'will be', but 'is' the Christ.

Who does the Bible declare Jesus to be?

We will consider a few references to Jesus Christ to establish who He is said to be.

John 5:16-23: If the Jehovah's Witness believed these verses, even in the *NWT*, they would know who Jesus is. However they do not just believe their Bible, they believe what the Society has told them their Bible says. We need therefore to both be able to understand these Scriptures and explain them to the Witness.

From verse 16 we know that Jesus was being persecuted for healing on the Sabbath. In verse 17 Jesus makes a simple statement – 'My Father.' From this the Jews understood that Jesus was claiming to be equal with God (v.18). This is very straightforward but the Witness has been taught that this is the unbelieving Jew who is calling Jesus 'God' and we should not believe what the unbelieving Jew says! Jesus had a way of saying the most profound things so that no one could understand Him (e.g. the parable of the Sower – Matt. 13). But here He spoke plainly so that the people understood. Jesus was also a Jew and understood how the Jewish mind worked. He knew that when He said, 'My Father' the Jews would understand that He was claiming to be, of the same substance as Jehovah, that is, God.

If Jesus is not equal with God who is at fault-Jesus for misleading them or the Jews for believing what Jesus was saying? Of course in these circumstances, Jesus would be at fault. This would make Him a liar and a fraud. This is not true; therefore, the statement must be correct. It is also very clear that the Jews were not unbelieving, they believed what Jesus said but rejected it.

John 20:28: This is the second time that Jesus has appeared to the disciples but the first time that Thomas has seen Him. His immediate response is to acknowledge Jesus as 'my Lord and my God.' Again this seems fairly clear until we realise that the Witness has been taught that either Thomas got so excited he blasphemed or he said 'my Lord' looking at Jesus and 'My God' looking up to Jehovah in heaven.

It clearly says 'Thomas said to Him' (Jesus) both statements. Secondly, ask the Witness what the *KIT* shows for the words Thomas used. He said *ho theos*, the phrase that the Society uses exclusively of Jehovah God. Jesus is called not just 'a god' but 'the God.' Thomas literally says, 'the God of me.' If this statement were not true, Jesus would have had to rebuke Thomas. However, in verse 29, He commends all those who will believe the same as Thomas believed.

In the midst of those who would go out to teach the early church, Jesus accepts the acclamation that He was God. What would the apostles believe? What must we also believe from this incident?

Rev. 5:13 & 14: Here Jesus is in His heavenly ministry. Who is receiving this honour, glory and worship? The One on the throne (Jehovah) and the Lamb (Jesus). Are we not to do what heaven is doing?

A Witness might say something like, 'only because Jesus was standing next to Jehovah does it appear that when they bow down to Jehovah – they are bowing down to Jesus'! Check verse 8, where they bow down to Jesus without Jehovah.

In addition, note that 'every creature' gives this to Jesus, who therefore cannot be a created being. This means that I cannot believe the Bible *and* the Watchtower; which one do I choose? The Society says that Jesus is Michael the Archangel, a created being. If this is true there is idol worship in heaven because creature would be worshipping creature. No angels, except the fallen ones, nor any other heavenly creatures, ever receive worship. Jesus, therefore, must be God.

Worship or obeisance?

The Witness will seek to make a distinction about the heavenly creatures, saying they were only doing obeisance to Jesus and that would be acceptable. In the whole of the New Testament it is the same Greek word, but the Watchtower will translate it as 'obeisance' referring to Jesus and 'worship' referring to Jehovah. In their minds the Witnesses think this is enough but note the following:

> When the Gentile Cornelius bowed reverently to the apostle Peter, note what happened: 'As Peter entered Cornelius met him fell down at his feet and did obeisance to him. But Peter lifted him up, saying, "Rise; I myself am also a man".' (Acts 10:25,26). BOWING WORSHIPFULLY to a human was improper, and Peter would not accept it. (*WT*, 1 May 1989, p. 22)

One human doing obeisance to another human is bowing WORSHIPFULLY and is wrong. In the same way one heavenly creature doing obeisance, bowing WORSHIPFULLY, to another would also be wrong.

Is Jesus God?

No comparison of Jesus in the light of Watchtower teaching would be complete without a mention of John 1:1. This verse probably causes more problems than any other. To show that Jesus is not God the *NWT* translates it, '... and the Word was a god ... ' Indeed it appears to provide ample evidence to prove that this is the correct translation. Here we examine this evidence.

Between 1962 and 1983 the WBTS quoted Johannes Greber to support its rendering of John 1:1, even though they knew in 1956 that his wife acted as a spirit medium to produce the translation. Why does the Watchtower translation agree with a spiritist Bible and why did 'God's organisation' knowingly use it as a reliable source for many years? (For more detailed information see Reachout Trust's booklet, *The Truth Revealed*). We will look here at the article from *Reasoning* and an article in *KIT*, p. 1139, that dealt with this subject.

Besides the attempt to find scholarly evidence, the Society's main defence for its translation is:

> John 1:18 says: 'No one has ever seen God.' Verse 14 clearly says that 'the Word became flesh and dwelt among us ... we have beheld his glory'. Also, verses 1, 2 say that in the beginning he was 'with God'. Can one be with someone and at the same time be that person? At John 17:3, Jesus addresses the Father as 'the only true God'; so, Jesus as 'a god' merely reflects his Father's divine qualities -Heb. 1:3. (*Reasoning*, p. 416)

This, as so many Watchtower arguments do, sounds convincing. Nevertheless, it is still an argument that is not backed up with the facts. The Watchtower argues that because the first 'God' in John 1:1 is preceded by the Greek definite article 'the' it must have a big 'G' and refer to Jehovah. However the second 'god' does not have the definite article and so is translated 'a god', and refers to the 'little god', Jesus.

What most Jehovah's Witnesses have not seen, however, is that in John 1:18 there is no definite article connected with the first *theon*[1] translated 'God', but the second *theos*[1] is followed by the definite article 'the one' and yet it is translated 'god.' When you add to this the meaning of the term 'only-begotten' (see p. 82) this verse says no man has ever seen God but now God the unique Son, clothed in flesh, reveals God in a way that can be seen by men.

John 1:14 is translated 'had a view of' in the *NWT*, instead of 'we viewed'. 'His glory' is rendered as 'a glory such as'. Both phrases are designed to lessen the impact of this verse, which means we saw the glory that is unique to God being begotten in the flesh.

The Society also uses an argument that speaks of Jesus being 'with' God and then asks 'how can He also be God?' This does not stand the test of comparing Scripture with Scripture.

The Father is God, and Jesus is God. Therefore, Jesus the Word was with God, but that does not make Him any less part of the Godhead. To check this out look at Heb. 1:3.

The *NWT* translates that Jesus is the 'reflection of' His Father and argues that you are not the same as your reflection! But the Greek word is *apaugasma*, literally translated in the *KIT* as 'beaming forth from.' Light beams forth from a torch and that is not a reflection, joy beams forth from a face and that is not a reflection, it is what is in the person coming out. The AV uses 'effulgence', more modern translations 'radiance', and that is exactly what the word means: not looking at a reflection in the mirror but a shining out from that which is within. This is underlined by the next phrase, 'the exact representation of his very being.' Jesus is not a pale reflection but from His very being shines forth that which He is, God.

Reasoning adds a few more points, most of which are dealt with in Chapter 7, and then refers the reader to the 1984 reference edition of the *NWT*. This article is the same as the one we will look at in the *KIT*.

We should note here that occasionally the Watchtower finds a new translation or 'scholar' to quote regarding its translation of John 1:1. Most, as the ones below show, whether knowingly or ignorantly, are misquoted. Whatever new illustrations are used the heart of the argument is the same. If you discover new references being used, please let us know so that they can be checked, too.

The Kingdom Interlinear Translations of the Greek Scriptures (1985, pp. 1139-40)

This article lists eight versions of the Bible that, the Society claims, support its 'a god' translation. As one of them is the *NWT* itself, we are left with seven to investigate.

1. The New Testament, in An Improved Version, Upon the Basis of Archbishop Newcome's New Translation: with a corrected text.

The name of Archbishop Newcome is supposed to lend weight but read carefully; it is an 'improved' version. However, that is a matter of opinion. Newcome's text, originally published in Dublin in 1796, reads, '... the Word was God.' The version quoted by the WBTS was published in London in 1808 and was the work of the Unitarians. Many of the footnotes in the translation indicate Newcome's original text but not at John 1:1. The Watchtower is not quoting Archbishop Newcome but the Unitarians, who we would expect to agree with the Society, as they also deny the deity of Christ.

2. The Monotessaron; or, The Gospel History, According to the Four Evangelists (J. S. Thompson, 1829).

Thompson translated this verse, '... and the Logos was a god ...' However, what is of interest is his actual meaning. This is shown by pages 32 and 33 of his pamphlet, *A Second Vindication of the Deity, and Atonement of Jesus* (1816):

> The words *theos en o logos* which are translated 'the word was God' are equally strong ... if the want of the article before *theos* NULLIFY THE DEITY OF THE SON IT ALSO DISPROVES THE DEITY OF THE FATHER in the 12th and 18th verses of this chapter. Moreover Dr Middleton has shown that the pure construction Greek Language requires that *theos* be put

without the article ... But lest any should conclude that this rule tends to prove Jesus the Supreme God, i.e. Father, I observe, that though Dr M[iddleton]'s rule be general, it is by no means universa l... Perhaps some may ask, are you not here disproving what you designed to prove? I answer no, both the text and criticism combine to ASSERT CHRIST'S DEITY; but at the same time, to deny Polytheism.

In the light of the above, his translation may be unwise, but what He means is evident, and it certainly is not what the Jehovah's Witness wants it to mean. There can be no doubt what Thompson believes as he wrote, in the same pamphlet:

I do most solemnly declare, that I firmly believe the following Articles ... 1. There is one Almighty ... God ... 2. The persons denominated Father, Son and Holy Ghost, Matt 28:19, ARE REALLY AND ESSENTIALLY GOD ... 3. The Lord Jesus Christ, the eternal Logos, exists before all worlds, begotten of the Father, NOT MADE, VERY GOD OF VERY GOD. (p. 9)

3. The Emphatic Diaglott (Benjamin Wilson).

The Society is honest enough to say that 'and a god was the Word' is the interlinear reading, not Wilson's final translation. Much has been written about Wilson being a Christadelphian and, be that as it may, we seem to miss the fact that he translated the verse, '... and the Logos was God.' The Society has been devious here. The interlinear is a word-for-word translation and as a word-for-word translation 'a god' is a possibility because there is no indefinite article ('a' or 'an') in Greek. Therefore, theos could be 'God', 'god', 'a God' or 'a god'. However, Wilson does not leave it as a literal translation but goes on to translate it with its proper full meaning as shown from the context of the passage, 'Logos was God.'

4. The Bible; An American Translation (J. M. P. Smith and E. J. Goodspeed).

This translation does not say 'a god' but, 'and the Word was divine'. I will leave comment on this to Bruce M. Metzger of Princeton Theological Seminary:

> As regards Jn 1:1, Colwell's research casts the most serious doubts on the correctness of such translations as 'and the Logos was divine' (Moffatt Strachan), 'and the Word was divine' (Goodspeed), and (worst of all) 'and the Word was a god.' (*Expository Times*, Vol. 6, 1952, p. 125)

5. Das Evangelium nach Johannes (Siegfrid Schulz).

Although the Society claims that Schulz said, 'and a god (or, of a divine kind) was the Word', he actually said 'and a God (or, God by nature) was the Word.' Either the German translators are not up to standard or this is deception. Schulz also said on pp. 18-19 of his commentary:

> God-ness characterizes the essence both of the 'Word' and of God himself. The word 'God' in the statement of v. 1.c. is not the subject – hence Luther's translation: 'God was the Word' – but the sentence predicate. The 'Word' is not 'the God' (thus v. 1b), i.e. God the Father. Nevertheless, the Logos is God by nature, of Godly being, identical in essence with God, so that the appropriate translation is: 'and of Godly nature was the Word.' (translated from the German)

6. Das Evangelium nach Johannes (Johannes Schneider).

This is a true translation: 'and godlike sort was the Logos.' Schneider, who was a Baptist, is now dead and all efforts to discover why he made this translation have so far failed.

7. *Das Evangelium nach Johannes (Jurgen Becker).*

Becker actually wrote, 'and a God was the Word.' We have in our possession a letter dated 24 July 1984 (see translation below) from Jurgen Becker who is Professor of New Testament at Kiel University.

> The first part of the verse makes the following statements: First, it is stated that the Logos (the Word) is not part of creation but belongs on the side of God. 'In the beginning' reminds us of Genesis 1:1. This is intentional and is usual in the context of statements relating to the role of wisdom as a mediator in creation... As a rule the creation of wisdom or of the Logos is said to be before all time... The text does not look back beyond the time of creation. Verse 1 does not speculate about pre-creation things but comments that the world, which we know (v. 3), owes its being to the mediatory role of the Logos in creation who was already with God before the world came into being (v.1). Concerning your discussion with the Jehovah's Witness I can therefore confirm that the JEHOVAH WITNESS INCORRECTLY CITE ME AS THEIR SOURCE. In my view, John 1:1 does not speak of the creation of the Logos but rather THE LOGOS WAS ALREADY IN EXISTENCE AT THE TIME OF CREATION.

All this apparent evidence amounts to very little. Out of the seven only two use 'a god,' and one of these is a perversion of Newcome's translation. One German translation is very little evidence compared with at least twenty English translations, apart from foreign editions, that can be quoted as saying 'God'.

The Society called upon Becker and Schulz again, along with three other German translations by Jeremais Felbinger, Oskar Holtzmann and Friedrich Rittelmyer. It mentions these five in an article entitled, *The 'New World Translation' Scholarly and Honest,* as follows:

But John 1:1 is not falsified in order to prove that Jesus is not Almighty God. Jehovah's Witnesses, among many others, had challenged the capitalizing of 'god' long before the appearance of the *New World Translation*, which endeavours accurately to render the original language. Five German Bible translators likewise use the term 'a god' in that verse. (*WT*, 1 March 1991)

The above quote is not found in the German translation of *The Watchtower* because every German would know that the evidence quoted here does not mean a thing. All German nouns have to start with a capital letter and so even if the 'a' is before it the translation could just as easily be a God. The Watchtower admitted that it had to make a choice in a letter from the British headquarters that reads in part:

Just as translators of the Greek manuscript which was written in all capitals have to make a choice on the way to present a translation that conveys the same meaning in their language, we have endeavoured to do this when translating from German into English.

As we have already shown there is plenty of evidence from Schulz and Becker to show what it meant, but of course it is easier for the Society to ignore that and put what it wants.

In a further effort to sound convincing the Society make much of the fact that the first *theos* has the definite article and the second does not. It quotes one authority in support, *Journal of Biblical Literature*, Vol. 92, pp. 75-87, P. B. Harner.

Some of the article is quoted correctly but the Society omits much of the flow of Harner's argument as to the best way to translate this clause. The concluding thoughts seem to sum up Harner's views; 'Perhaps this clause could be translated, "the Word had the same nature as God."' This, of course, is not what the Witnesses would want it to say.

Having checked the evidence, and seen that most of it does

not support the Witnesses claims, we end this section with two quotes from Greek scholars. The second is of real interest to the Society as it is by B. F. Westcott whose Greek text it uses.

It needs to be recognized that the Fourth Evangelist need not have chosen the word-order, and that his choice of it, though creating some ambiguity, may in itself be an indication of his meaning ... Westcott's note ... 'it IS NECESSARILY WITHOUT THE ARTICLE (*theos* not *ho theos*) inasmuch as it describes the nature of the Word and does not identify His person. (C. F. D. Moule, *An Idiom Book of New Testament Greek*, 1953, p. 116)

The three clauses contain all that is possible for man to realise as to the essential nature of the Word in relation to time, and mode of being, and character: He was (1) 'in the beginning': He was (2) 'with God': He was (3) 'God' ... the Word was God. The predicate (*theos*) stands emphatically first, as in 4:24. It is necessarily without the article (*theos* not *o theos*) inasmuch as it describes the nature of the Word and does not identify His person. It would be pure Sabellianism [Unitarianism] to say 'the Word was *o theos*.' No idea of inferiority of nature is suggested by the form of expression, which simply affirms the true deity of the Word ... in the third clause 'the Word' is declared to be 'God', and so included in the unity of the Godhead. Thus we are led to conceive that the divine nature is essentially in the Son, and at the same time the Son can be regarded, according to that which is His peculiar characteristics, in relation to God as God. (B. F. Westcott, *The Gospel According to St John*, Vol. 1, 1908, pp. 4-6)

Conclusion
How different is the Jesus of Scripture from the one portrayed in the Watchtower Bible and publications such as *The Greatest*

Man Who Ever Lived? Which one will the Witness believe in, the one in the Bible or the one in the Watchtower publication? The answer is made clear by *The Articles of Amendment to the Articles of Incorporation of Watch Tower Bible and Tract Society*. This document, dated January 1945, includes as part of the purpose of the Society in Article seven,

> ... and for public Christian WORSHIP of Almighty God and JESUS CHRIST.

The Watchtower knows about this document and tries to overcome the problem by misquoting its own official Articles,

> ... and for public Christian worship of Almighty God [through] Christ Jesus. (*WT*, 15 December 1971, pp. 759-60)

Note

1. A Witness might try to wriggle out of this by saying these are different words. Word endings do not change in English for male, female, neuter or for a different grammatical case but they do in many European languages. This is the same word with a different ending because of the different case it is in. (See confirmation of this in *WT*, 15 May 1977, p. 319)

6

The Godhead – Holy Spirit

— ☙ —

> God's Active Force; Holy Spirit ... Not a person. Not until the fourth century CE did the teaching that the holy spirit was a person and part of the 'Godhead' become official church dogma ... The Scriptures themselves unite to show that God's holy spirit is not a person but is God's active force by which he accomplishes his purpose and executes his will ... personification does not prove personality. (*Insight*, Vol. 2, p. 1019)

We need to check the Society's definition (above) with Scripture to see if there, long before the fourth century, we find that the Holy Spirit is a person not a force, likened to electricity; and that this person is the third member of the Godhead.

His personality

In an indirect way the Watchtower shows that the Holy Spirit is a person.

> Is the Devil a personification or a person?... these accounts relate to conversations between the Devil and God, and between the Devil and Jesus Christ. Both Jehovah God and Jesus Christ are persons. Can an unintelligent 'force' carry on a conversation with a person? Also, the Bible calls Satan a manslayer, a liar, a father (in spiritual sense) and a ruler... ONLY AN INTELLIGENT PERSON COULD FIT ALL THOSE DESCRIPTIONS. (*Aw.*, 8 December 1973, p. 27)

Here, concerning the Devil, personification *does* prove personality. We must therefore be able to take the same 'rules' and apply them to prove the personality of the Holy Spirit. First, Witnesses say the Devil has to be a person because he talks to other persons:

> So THE SPIRIT SAID to Philip ... (Acts 8:29, *NWT*)
> ... THE HOLY SPIRIT SAID ... (Acts 13:2, *NWT*)
> ... just as THE HOLY SPIRIT SAYS ... (Heb 3:7, *NWT*)

The Holy Spirit talks with other people; therefore, He cannot be an unintelligent force!

Secondly, the names Scripture gives to the Devil show he must be a person.

> But the HELPER, the HOLY SPIRIT, which the Father will send in my name, THAT ONE WILL TEACH you all things... (John 14:26, *NWT*)
> However when that one arrives, the spirit of the truth, HE WILL GUIDE you into all the truth; for he will not SPEAK of his own impulse, but whatever things he HEARS HE WILL SPEAK... (John 16:13, *NWT*)

The Holy Spirit is a helper, a teacher, a guide, a speaker and a hearer, all of which clearly show that He is an intelligent person.

One name especially, 'helper' gives us a clear insight into His person. The Greek word is *parakletos* and this is what Greek scholar W. E. Vine says about the word:

> ... lit., called to one's side, i.e., to one's aid, is primarily a verbal adjective, and suggests the capability or adaptability for giving aid. It was used in a court of justice to denote a legal assistant, counsel for the defence, an advocate; then, generally, of one who pleads another's cause, an intercessor, advocate, as in 1 John 2:1, of the Lord Jesus. In the widest sense, it signifies a succourer, com-

forter. Christ was to His disciples, by implication of His word 'another (*allos*, another of the same sort, not *heteros* different) Comforter,' when speaking of the Holy Spirit, John 14:16. In John 14:26;15:26;16:7 He calls Him 'the Comforter'. (*Vine*, Vol. 1, p. 208)

With this one description, Vine has encapsulated so much proof of the person of the Holy Spirit. First, the definition of *parakletos* shows such a one who pleads and aids must be an intelligent person. Secondly, he shows that both the Lord Jesus and the Holy Spirit are called the *parakletos*. Third, he underlines the use of the word *allos* for 'another' which clearly means of the same sort, not different. These last two points link the Holy Spirit and Jesus together as beings of the same sort, that is, intelligent persons.

Besides the Witnesses' own definition, there are other indications that the Holy Spirit is a person. However, before we look at them we should mention one comeback that you might receive from a Witness. They are taught in *Reasoning*, p. 380, that just because something is personified it does not mean it is a person, and 'wisdom' is given as an illustration. If you ever hear this remember the following quote, that turns this argument on its head

God's Son had a fondness for mankind even during his pre-human existence. UNDER THE FIGURE OF WISDOM PERSONIFIED, HE IS IDENTIFIED as God's 'master worker' . . . (*WT*, 15 April 1980, p. 26)

Wisdom personified is the person of Jesus! The Holy Spirit personified is the person of the Holy Spirit. There are, however, other indications in Scripture.

He has the characteristics of a person

Four characteristics are only ever found in intelligent persons. They are never found in things. The Holy Spirit is shown to have these qualities:

- Intelligence – John 14:26 – ability to teach.
- A mind – Rom. 8:27.
- A will -1 Cor. 12:11.
- Affections – Eph. 4:30 – an unintelligent force cannot feel grief!

In John 14:17 the *NWT* refers to the Holy Spirit as an 'it' and in the strict grammatical sense this is right because the Greek word for spirit, *pneuma*, is neuter and therefore the pronouns that refer to it are also in the neuter. However, even the WBTS has to call the Holy Spirit 'he' in John 16:13 where we have the neuter *pneuma* and the masculine *ekinos*. Vine sums this up:

> THE PERSONALITY OF THE HOLY SPIRIT IS EMPHASIZED at the expense of strict grammatical procedure in John 14:26;15:26;16:813,14, where the emphatic pronoun *eikeinos*, 'He,' is used of Him in the masculine, whereas the noun *pneuma* is neuter ... (*Vine*, Vol. 4, p. 64)

He has the characteristics of God

Just as there are certain characteristics only found in a person so there are also certain characteristics only found in God. The Scriptures show the Holy Spirit to have these characteristics:

- Omnipresence – Ps. 139:7-10 – only God is present every-where.
- All knowing – Is. 40:13-14 – no one taught Him.
- Sovereign – 1 Cor. 12:11- only God can do just as He chooses.
- Eternal – Heb. 9:14.

He does the work of God

- Creation – Job 33:4, Ps. 104:30 (these verses should be read with Is. 44:24 where Jehovah says, I alone, Myself created).
- Regeneration – John 3:5,6, Tit. 3:5.
- Sanctification – Rom. 15:16, 1 Cor. 6:11, 2 Thess. 2:13, 1 Pet. 1:1-2.
- Resurrection – Rom. 8:11.

There are other important verses. Acts 5:3-4, even in the *NWT*, indicates clearly that the Holy Spirit is God.

> Acts 5:3 – ' ... play false to the holy spirit ... '
> Acts 5:4 – ' ... played false ... to God ... '

Most Christians are more used to the translation 'lied to,' and it is impossible to lie to an active force!

Finally 2 Cor. 3:16-18,

> But when there is a turning to Jehovah, the veil is taken away. NOW JEHOVAH IS THE SPIRIT; and where the spirit of Jehovah is, there is freedom. And all of us, while we with unveiled faces reflect like mirrors the glory of Jehovah, are transformed into the same image from glory to glory, exactly as done by JEHOVAH [THE] SPIRIT. (*NWT*)

Conclusion

Truly, the Scriptures show beyond any doubt that the Holy Spirit is a person and is God.

7

The Godhead – The Trinity

— ை —

The Father – The Trinity

In chapter 5 we saw that the WBTS teaches that the Father alone is God and that therefore there can be no Trinity. We have also seen in chapters 6 and 7 that the Scriptures show that Jesus and the Holy Spirit are God and that shows that the Trinity is not pagan. However, the Society still believes that history shows that the doctrine of the Trinity is man-made and pagan.

The Watchtower has produced a booklet concerning the Trinity and its pagan origins entitled *Should you Believe in the Trinity*. Reachout Trust has answered this publication in detail with its publication, *Why Should you Believe 'Should you Believe in the Trinity'?* Here we will look briefly at some aspects of this subject using the article on the Trinity found in *Reasoning*, which covers some twenty pages (405-426). First, we will check some of the publications that the WBTS calls on to support its assertions about the Trinity. *Reasoning* left out the parts in bold print when it used the quotations.

> Neither the word Trinity, nor the explicit doctrine as such, appears in the New Testament, nor did Jesus and his followers intend to contradict the Shema in the Old Testament: 'Hear, O Israel: The Lord our God is one Lord' (Deut. 6:4). **The earliest Christians, however, had to cope with the implications of the coming of Jesus Christ and of the presence and power of God among**

them i.e., The Holy Spirit, whose coming we connected with the celebration of Pentecost. The Father, Son, and Holy Spirit were associated in such New Testament passages as the Great Commission: 'Go therefore and make disciples of all nations, baptizing them in the name of The Father and of the Son and of the Holy Spirit' (Mt. 28:19); and in the apostolic benediction: 'The grace of the Lord Jesus Christ and the love of God and the fellowship of the Holy Spirit be with you all' (2 Cor 13:14). Thus, the New Testament established the basis for the doctrine of the Trinity. The doctrine developed gradually over several centuries and through many controversies ... By the end of the 4th century ... the doctrine of the Trinity took substantially the form it has maintained ever since. (*EB* Vol. X, 1976, p. 126)

It is difficult, in the second half of the 20th century to offer a clear, objective, and straightforward account of the ... Trinity ... Among the Apostolic Fathers, Clement of Rome ... in the final decade of the 1st century, bears witness to God the Father, to the Son, to the Spirit ... From what has been seen thus far, the impression could arise that the Trinitarian dogma is in the last analysis a late 4th century invention. In a sense, this is true; but it implies an extremely strict interpretation on the key words Trinitarian and dogma. The formulation 'one God in three Persons' was not solidly established, certainly not fully assimilated into Christian life and its profession of faith, prior to the end of the 4th century. But it is precisely this formulation that has first claim to the title the Trinitarian dogma. Among the Apostolic Fathers, there had been nothing even remotely approaching such a mentality or perspective. (*NCE*, Vol. XIV, 1967, pp. 295-99)

What the Society omits to tell its readers about the following quote is that it comes from an eight-page article on 'Unitarianism.' Unitarians are a group who openly deny both the deity of Christ and that Christ died for our sins. The part of the article we have added from p. 301 shows this clearly.

> Christianity derived from Judaism and Judaism was strictly Unitarian (believing that God is one person). The road which led from Jerusalem to Nicea was scarcely a straight one. Fourth-century Trinitarianism did not reflect accurately early Christian teaching regarding the nature of God; it was, on the contrary, a deviation from this teaching ... **The alleged fact that Jesus died for our sins, and thus guarded us against the effects of the wrath of God, is categorically denied. To believe that Jesus' death did have this result would be to cast an aspersion on God's character ... Moreover, man should not, Unitarians believe, accept such an offer on the part of Jesus ...** (*EA*, Vol. XXVII, 1956, p. 294L)

The Society is guilty of quoting an anti-Christian group to try to 'prove' its erroneous doctrines.

> The trinity of persons within the unity of nature is defined in terms of 'person' and 'nature' which are G[ree]k philosophical terms; actually the terms do not appear in the Bible. The Trinitarian definitions arose as the result of long controversies in which these terms and others such as 'essence' and 'substance' were erroneously applied to God by some theologians ... **This distinction between God and flesh is the NT basis for the affirmation of the unity of nature; the very identification of the Father with 'the God' shows that the NT writers intended to distinguish the Son and the Spirit from the Father. The NT does not approach the metaphysical problem of subordination as it approaches no**

metaphysical problem. It offers no room for a statement of the relations of Father, Son and Spirit which would imply that one of them is more or less properly on the divine level of being than another ... any statement of this distinction which reduces the divinity of any of the persons is a false statement. (John L. McKenzie, *Dictionary of the Bible*, 1965, pp. 899-900)

Although the NT concepts of the Spirit of God are largely a continuation of those of the OT, in the NT there is a gradual revelation that the Spirit of God is a Person. In the Synoptic Gospels. The majority of N[ew] T[estament] texts reveal God's spirit as something not someone; This is especially seen in the parallelism between the spirit and the power of God. *(NCE, Vol. XIII, 1967, p. 575)*

The God of the Christian, like the God of the Israelites, was unequivocally one. Nevertheless if as Justin notes (1 Apol. 13), Christians worship Christ in the second place and the Spirit in the third place, there is still no inconsistency; for the Word and Spirit are not to be separated from the unique Godhead of the Father ... The Apologists [Greek Christian writers of the second century] spoke too haltingly of the Spirit; with a measure of anticipation, one might say too impersonally. (*NCE*, Vol. XIV, 1967, p. 296)

Theos (God) is still never used of the Spirit .... there are six complete texts in which *o theos* is used to speak of the Second Person of the Trinity ... *O theos* (literally, the God) is never used in the New Testament to speak of the 'holy spirit'. (Karl Rahner, Vol. 1, *Theological Investigations*, 1961, pp. 138, 143)

McClintock and Strong's *Cyclopedia of Biblical, Theological, and Ecclesiastical Literature*, though advocating the Trinity doctrine, acknowledges: 'This text [Matt. 28:18-20], however, taken by itself, would not prove decisively either the personality of the three subjects mentioned, or their equality or divinity' (1981 reprint, Vol. X, p. 552). Regarding other texts that also mention the three together, this *Cyclopedia* admits that, taken by themselves, they are 'insufficient' to prove the Trinity. (Compare 1 Timothy 5:21, where God and Christ and the angels are mentioned together.)

The Society only refers to this book without quoting in full because these scholars actually say the opposite!

> The first class of texts taken by itself, proves only that there are three subjects named and that there is a difference between them; that the Father in certain respects differs from the Son, etc.; but it does not prove, by itself, that all three belong necessarily to the divine nature and possess equal divine honour. **In proof of this, the second class of texts must be addressed ... These texts prove (a) that the Son and Holy Spirit, according to the doctrine of the New Test[ament], are divine, or belong to the one divine nature; and (b) that the three subjects are personal and equal.** (*ibid.* p. 552)

These scholars do not say the Trinity is of pagan origin, nor that it is not found in the Bible, in fact just the opposite. How can the Society, which calls itself God's channel of truth, twist things so much?

The fact that the Trinity 'dogma' was not written down until the fourth century is true. The reason, though, is not that it was only invented then but that this truth, believed and taught in the early church, came under severe attack at that time. The truth had not been questioned so fiercely before and had never needed to be defined 'on paper.' Now Christians wanted everyone to know what they believed. This aspect is dealt with in more detail in *Why Should you Believe 'Should you Believe in the Trinity'?*

The quotes above show that scholars do not agree with the Society's teaching, but remember we can never understand the Trinity with our minds. The divine relationship of the Godhead (incidentally, because the word 'Trinity' is like a red rag to a bull it is usually better to use 'Godhead') can only be grasped by the Holy Spirit witnessing to our spirits. This is a great disadvantage to Jehovah's Witnesses and even after hours of sharing many will not change their views, because the enemy blinds them.

There are several Scriptures however that can be looked at in a different light to the one that the Society gives.

John 1. Verses 1 and 2, are dealt with on pp. 416-17 of *Reasoning.* The Greek aspects of these verses are dealt with elsewhere but let us look at the context.

Verse 1: 'In the beginning,' the Greek phrase for this is the same as the Greek translation (Septuagint) for Gen. 1:1. When the beginning begun God was there and now when the beginning begun the Word, Christ was there. Neither of them was created and both were in existence before any creation took place. Heb. 7:3, even in the *NWT*, shows that the Son of God had no 'beginning of days nor an end of life,' He is eternal.

Verse 3: All things created by Him. The Word of God offers no exceptions as the emphasis in this verse shows: 'apart from Him nothing came into being.' Only if you bring human interpretation to bear can you say that Christ was created.

Verse 14: Only-begotten. The Greek word *monogenes* is contrasted with the word for born, *gennao* in verse 13. Christ is the unique one, not born as we are, but begotten. Begotten can never mean created.

> We don't use the words begetting or begotten much in modern English, but everyone still knows what they mean. To beget is to become the father of: to create is to make. And the difference is just this. When you beget,

you beget something of the same kind as yourself. A man begets human babies, a beaver begets little beavers, and a bird begets eggs which turn into little birds. But when you make, you make something of a different kind from yourself ... What God begets is God; just as what man begets is man. What God creates is not God; just as what man makes is not man. That is why men are not Sons of God in the sense that Christ is. (C. S. Lewis, *Beyond Personality*, 1944, p. 12)

We can only rightly understand the term 'the only begotten' when used of the Son, in the sense of unoriginated relationship.

The begetting is not an event of time, however remote, but a fact irrespective of time. The Christ did not become, but necessarily and eternally is the Son. He, a Person, possesses every attribute of pure Godhood. This necessitates eternity, absolute being; in this respect he is not 'after' the Father'. (*Vine*, Vol. 3, p. 140)

Reasoning, pp. 416-24 mentions several other verses under the revealing heading, 'Texts from which a person might draw more than one conclusion, depending on the Bible translation used'. We list these texts and add a few comments.

John 8:58. The Society cannot accept that Jesus is the 'I AM,' so He becomes the 'I have been.' It tries to justify this with a quote from A. T. Robertson, but even he says this is impossible:

The Progressive Present. This is a poor name in lieu of a better one for the present of a past action STILL IN PROGRESS ... In John 8:58 *eimi* is really absolute. (A. T. Robertson, *A Grammar of the Greek New Testament in the Light of Historical Research*, p. 879)

There is however a very interesting verse in the *NWT* to be mentioned here.

> This is the one about whom I said, Behind me there comes a man who has advanced in front of me, because HE EXISTED BEFORE ME (John 1:30, *NWT*)

In this life Jesus never existed before John, He must have existed as Jesus eternally.

Acts 20:28. As there is a great debate among scholars as to whether the phrase here is 'church of God' or 'church of the Lord', it does not seem helpful to pursue this issue. We do not need to anyway, with so much other clear evidence.

Rom. 9:5. The punctuation is changed in the *NWT* so that Christ is not equated with God. It quotes from the *International Dictionary of New Testament Theology* (Vol. 2, p. 80), but ends the quote before this part on the next page:

> ... the passage cannot be treated as a doxology to God the Father, since it does not follow the form of doxologies elsewhere in the LXX and the NT. The application of *theos* to Christ suits the context ... comparable assertions of divinity may be found in 2 Thess. 1:2; Tit. 2:13; Phil. 2:6; Col. 2:9; and 2 Cor. 3:17 ... 'God blessed for evermore' stands in apposition to Christ.

Again, the Society tampers with the Word of God without evidence.

Phil. 2:5-6. Witnesses argue that Christ can not be equal to God and, as usual, have a scholar who appears to agree with them, but the quote continues:

Are we not obliged then, to think of the [Greek] *harpagman* (= *harpagma*) as something still future ... Observe how aptly the view fits the context. In verse 10, which is the climax of the whole passage, we read that God gave Jesus Christ as a gift ... the name above every name, i.e. the name (including position, dignity and authority) of *kyrios*, Lord, the name which represents the OT Jehovah. But this is the highest place Christ has reached. He has always (in Paul's view) shared the Divine nature ... But it is only as the result of His Incarnation, Atonement, Resurrection and Exultation that He appears to men as on an equality with God, that He is worshipped by them in the way which Jehovah is worshipped. (*The Expositor's Greek Testament*, 1967, edited by W. Robertson Nicoll, Vol. III, p. 437)

We must thank the Society for giving us this quote to show that Jesus is God.

Col. 2:9. The Witnesses' argument that the Greek here is not to be translated 'Godhead,' but 'divine quality,' is full of Watchtower logic but not scriptural content. I think the answer lies in what Vine says:

> *theiotes* ... divinity ... is to be distinguished from *theotes*, in Colossians 2:9, 'Godhead' ... [in this passage] Paul is declaring that in the Son there dwells all the fullness of absolute Godhead; they were no mere rays of Divine glory which gilded Him, lighting up His Person for a season and with a splendour not His own; but He was, and is, absolute and perfect God. (*Vine*, Vol. 1, pp. 328-29)

The Society claims 'Clearly therefore, the Scriptures do not support the idea of "the divinity of Christ"' (*WT*, 15 January 1922,

p. 23). Yet Col. 2:9 reads in the *KIT*, 1985 edition 'Because in him dwells the fullness of the divinity' (Literal English translation).

Tit. 2:13. This verse is changed to stop it reading that Jesus is God. But the scholarly quote has the ending missed off.

> ... **Whichever way taken, the passage is just as important testimony to the divinity of our Saviour: according to (1) (Jesus Christ, the great God and our Saviour), by asserting His possession of Deity and right to the appellation of the Highest: according to (2) (the great God and of our Saviour, Jesus Christ), even more strikingly, asserting His equality in glory with the Father** ... (H. Alford, *The Greek Testament*, 1877, p. 421)

In other words, whichever way you translate it, Jesus is equal with the Father, God!

Heb. l:8. Another classic misquotation:

> ... In whatever way then *o theos* be taken, the quotation establishes the conclusion which the writer wishes to draw as to the essential difference of the Son and angels. Indeed it might appear to many that the direct application of the divine Name to the Son would obscure this thought. (B. F. Westcott, *The Epistle to the Hebrews*, 1889, p. 26)

Westcott's position is made clear on p. 20 of the same book:

> **Nor is it without the deepest significance that in the fundamental passages, Ps[alm] 2:7, 2 Sam[uel] 7:14 the speaker is 'the Lord' and not 'God': The unique**

title of Christ is thus connected with God as He is God of the Covenant (*Jehovah, the* Lord).

Old Testament posers for Jehovah's Witnesses

Mal. 3:1. This verse and footnote in *NWT*, 1971 large-print edition, gives the Witness all sorts of problems.

> 'Look! I am sending my messenger, and he must clear up a way before me. And suddenly there will certainly come to His temple the (true) Lord, whom you people are seeking, and the messenger of the covenant in whom you are delighting. Look! He will certainly come,' Jehovah of armies has said. (*NWT*)

Clearly, Jehovah is speaking about the true Lord whom He will send. The true Lord whom the people are seeking and the only one ever to come to the temple, is Jesus. The footnote says that the Hebrew for 'true lord' is *ha-Adon* and cites eight other occurrences of the word. The 1970 *NWT* (p. 1455) explains further that *ha-Adon* is only ever used of Jehovah God. Every one of these Scriptures links the name Jehovah with true Lord, usually as 'the true Lord, Jehovah.' Every one, except Mal. 3:1! If the Society did that here the verse would say that Jehovah was sending Jehovah, but, more devastating, it would show that Christ is the true Lord, Jehovah.

The *WT*, 15 June 1987 tried to answer this problem by saying 'After having mentioned one messenger, Malachi indicated that "the true Lord" would come to "His temple" accompanied by another, a different messenger, "the messenger of the covenant".' (p. 12)

But wait, Mal. 3:1 does not mention two distinct persons; 'And suddenly there will come to His temple the true Lord, whom you are seeking, and the messenger of the covenant in whom you are delighting.' (*NWT*) This is one and the same person. How can we be so sure? The verse ends 'Look! He will certainly come, Jehovah of armies has said.'

First note that 'He' not 'they' will come and note that Jehovah says that 'He will come' not 'I will come'.

This explanation gets even worse because, having said that Jehovah and Jesus are coming to the Temple, the Watchtower then says,

> 'The true Lord' Jehovah did not come personally to the literal temple in Jerusalem. (1 Kings 8:27) He came representatively, that is, by means of his 'messenger of the covenant,' Jesus Christ, who came in Jehovah's name and with the backing of God's holy spirit. (*WT*, 15 June 1987, p. 12)

Right, now we know – only one person came to the temple, Jesus Christ, who is called the true Lord, the name reserved for Jehovah.

Zech. 2:10-12
> 'Cry out ... O daughter of Zion; for here I am coming, and I will reside in the midst of you,' is the utterance of Jehovah ... And you will have to know that Jehovah of armies himself has sent me to you. And Jehovah will... yet choose Jerusalem. (*NWT*)

It is clear that Jehovah is the one coming and residing in Jerusalem, not Zechariah as some Witnesses will try to say. However, it is also clear that Jehovah of armies has sent Him. A clear case of two 'Jehovahs' in the *NWT*. The only possible answer is that God the Father is sending God the Son.

Jer. 23:5-6
> 'Look! There are days coming,' is the utterance of Jehovah, 'and I will raise up to David a righteous sprout. And a king will certainly reign and act with discretion and execute justice and righteousness in the land. In his days Judah will be saved, and Israel itself will reside in

security. And this is his name with which he will be called, Jehovah Is Our Righteousness.' (*NWT*)

Jesus is called by the name of Jehovah!

New Testament posers for Jehovah's Witnesses

Which name?

And everyone who calls on the NAME OF JEHOVAH will be saved. (Acts 2:21, *NWT*)

... in the NAME OF JESUS CHRIST ... does this man stand here ... Furthermore, there is NO SALVATION IN ANYONE ELSE, for there is NOT ANOTHER NAME under heaven that has been given among men by which we must GET SAVED. (Acts 4:10-12, *NWT*)

To worship or not to worship?

Luke 4:8 makes it clear that only God must be worshipped. Yet, the Scriptures show that Jesus received worship. But not according to Heb. 1:6 in the *NWT*: 'let all God's angels do obeisance to him.'

The Watchtower's 'evolution' of Heb. 1:6 is interesting.

And let all God's angels WORSHIP him. (Heb 1:6, *NWT*, 1970)

In 1970 it was all right for Jesus to receive worship.

And let all God's angels DO OBEISANCE to him. (Heb 1:6, *NWT*, large print, 1971)

By 1971, Jehovah had changed His mind, or had He? The verse had a footnote, 'Or "worship him." Compare Heb. 11:21.' Jehovah was not sure! By the way, Heb. 11:21, which we must compare, is all about Jacob worshipping. Again, we find that the truth is there for any seeker to find. Jesus can and did receive worship, which means He is either a fraud or God.

There are two interesting sidelights to these verses of Heb. 1:6.

First, an article in *WT*, 15 January, 1992, p. 23 condemned translations that render this verse as 'worship.' Of course, it omitted to own up to the fact that it translated it like that for many years.

Secondly, although today a Jehovah's Witness must not worship Jesus, in 1916 they were told that many would worship Charles T. Russell:

> Charles Taze Russell, thou hast, by the Lord, been crowned a king ... and thy enemies shall come and WORSHIP at thy feet. (*ZWTR*, 1 December 1916, p. 6015)

Did they really believe that Russell was more important than Jesus was?

Problem verses for Christians

There are some verses about the person of Christ that Witnesses rely on and we need to understand them.

John 14:28. Jesus said His Father was greater than He was, therefore how can Jesus be God? The argument sounds logical and because the Witnesses rely so much on logic, they have problems. However, what does 'greater' mean? Better? Different than? The same Greek word is used in John 14:12: 'greater works you will do.' Are we going to do better or different works than Jesus? No, greater here simply means in more magnitude; they will be no better and certainly not different. The self-imposed limitations of Jesus' earthly life caused His Father to be greater only at that time and in that place. Incidentally, only things in the same magnitude can be compared. Jesus claimed equality and oneness with the Father, John 5:18; 10:30, and therefore could be compared with Him.

1 Cor. 15:28. There is always right subjection in the relationship between the Father and the Son (see John 5:30). Jesus willingly allows this and it does not imply that He is lesser than the Father. The word for subjection is a military term meaning to put in rank, a right order created to achieve a desired end which does not imply inequality. For instance, Luke 2:51 tells us that Jesus was in subjection to His parents. Did this make Him less than His parents? No, it was just the right order, which Jesus willingly accepted. Eph. 5:21 shows us this relationship in the body of Christ and verse 22 within marriage, but neither indicate that one has to be less than the other, simply that there is a right order.

8

Salvation

___ ༄ ___

The Watchtower's teaching on salvation is one of double standards. Ask a Witness if they believe in salvation by faith and they will honestly say 'yes'. However, asking the same Witness what would happen to them if they left the Society shows that in reality they believe that their salvation is in 'God's organisation'

The Society defines salvation as follows:

> Preservation or deliverance from danger or destruction. That deliverance may be from the hands of oppressors or persecutors. For all true Christians, Jehovah provides through his Son deliverance from the present wicked system of things as well as salvation from bondage to sin and death. For a great crowd of faithful servants of Jehovah living during 'the last days', salvation will include preservation through the great tribulation. (*Reasoning*, p. 356)

This sounds great, but the double standard appears when the above is compared with the following quotes:

> Remember, though, that you MUST WORK HARD to receive these blessings. It will COST YOU time and effort ... We therefore urge one and all to lay hold on God's promises and to trust him fully. By continued diligent study of the Bible and by application of its wise counsel you MAY

attain to the grandest of blessings, including everlasting life in a paradise earth! (*WT*, 1 July 1984, p. 6)

Salvation cannot be earned by attendance at meetings or in any other way. It is free, a gift from God. Yet, Jehovah God does REQUIRE EFFORTS on our part if we are TO RECEIVE his gift of everlasting life. (*WT*, 15 January 1986, p. 10)

This is like winning a 'free' holiday and finding when you go to collect it you have to pay hundreds of pounds for insurance! The gift is free but we must pay before we receive it.

It should not surprise us to find that the Witnesses' gospel of salvation is not the one of Scripture when we read:

But the Kingdom witnessing of Jehovah's Witnesses since 1914 has been something FAR DIFFERENT FROM what Christendom's missionaries have published both before and since 1914. (*WT*, 1 October 1980, p. 28)

Two examples of this 'far different' gospel appear in a Watchtower article on being 'born again'. First, it claims that Jesus was born again and those ruling with Him will be born again. Then it changes the scene to speak of the great crowd:

What about these anointed footstep followers of Jesus Christ? When are they 'born again'? What steps must they take before Jehovah acts on their behalf, bringing them forth as spiritual sons? ... There are SIX DISTINCT STEPS that these must take. But let it be noted that God requires these same things of all who would become true Christians and gain salvation ... To begin with, such persons must take in accurate knowledge about Jehovah God, their Creator and Life-Giver, and about his Son, Jesus Christ, their Savior and Redeemer ... A person must exercise faith ... The very first WORK that is required as proof of a person's faith is that of repentance... A person must take the step of conversion ... Then just as Jesus presented himself at the Jordan ... the next step required... is to present themselves to God. Today, this includes making a dedication to Jehovah God, after which they must follow in the footsteps of his Son, Jesus ... Further, as a sixth step they must symbolize this dedication and make an open confession of it by undergoing baptism ... (*WT*, 1 February 1982, pp. 25-26)

Only after taking all six steps will we gain salvation and as taking in knowledge and exercising faith are ongoing steps, we can never know if we have attained to the standard.

The definition of justification is also rewritten. To the Christian it is the glorious fact that we, who could never attain to God's righteous standard, are declared righteous by the work of the Lord Jesus and can therefore live in God's presence. To Jehovah's Witnesses it is the possibility that if they accomplish appropriate deeds during the millennium they will attain to perfection. (see *WT*, 1 December 1985, pp. 4-18)

Despite the Society's attempts to say otherwise, the definition of salvation in the Scriptures is clear and final: 'For by grace you HAVE BEEN saved through faith: and that NOT OF YOUR-SELVES, it is the GIFT of God; NOT AS A RESULT OF WORKS, that no one should boast.' (Eph 2:8-9)

The Society might pay lip service to this Biblical definition but a more appropriate version might be: 'For by grace you MIGHT YET BE saved through faith: and that MUST HAVE SOMETHING TO DO WITH YOURSELVES, it is NOT ENTIRELY THE GIFT of God; IT IS AS A RESULT OF WORKS, that we should boast in the Society.' (Eph 2:8-9, revised according to Watchtower doctrine)

The following quotations show where this definition comes from.

Jehovah God offers you something wonderful-everlasting life... you must have faith in Jehovah ... However, MORE THAN FAITH IS NEEDED. There must also be WORKS...

(*You can Live Forever in Paradise on Earth*, WBTS, 1982, p. 250)

What does God REQUIRE of those who will reside forever upon his Paradise earth? ... Jesus Christ identified a FIRST REQUIREMENT ... taking in knowledge ... Many have found the SECOND REQUIREMENT more difficult ... obey God's laws ... A THIRD REQUIREMENT is that we be associated with God's channe l... The FOURTH REQUIREMENT ... loyally advocating his Kingdom rule to others. (*WT*, 15 February 1983, pp. 2-13)

Though getting baptized is evidence that you are spiritually progressive, remember that baptism is just A BEGINNING STEP ... dedication may be compared to APPLYING FOR EVERLASTING LIFE in God's new system ... Afterward you must faithfully live up to your DEDICATION IN ORDER TO RECEIVE GOD'S GIFT OF EVERLASTING LIFE. (*WT*, 15 August 1957, p. 16)

What is your reaction to the resurrection hope? Jehovah will keep his promise to resurrect millions, even billions, from the dead. Whether you will be there to see them again, and be seen by them, DEPENDS LARGELY ON WHAT YOU DO. Are you willing to learn about and live in harmony with God's REQUIREMENTS FOR GAINING ETERNAL LIFE. (*WT*, 15 June 1992, p. 7)

Baptism
The above quotes show that baptism is an essential part of salvation for Jehovah's Witnesses. 'New light' on baptism over the years has taken the Society away from the truth.

Entrance into the body of Christ is not made on the basis of logic or philosophy, but is made on the basis of faith in Jesus Christ and whole hearted devotion to him. We think by far the better way, the scriptural way, is for the one who conducts the baptismal service, or the one who gives the Scriptural talk on such an occasion, to ask merely the simple questions: (1) Do you believe in Christ Jesus as your Redeemer, and your personal Saviour from sin and death? (2) Have you presented your heart and life to God, to follow the indications of his will under the headship of Jesus his Son? (*WT*, 1 February 1921, pp. 42-3)

Thirty-seven years later the questions had evolved away from Jesus and trust solely in Him.

It is essential that with the mouth public declaration of faith be made. Two questions are therefore asked the candidates: (1) Have you recognized yourself before Jehovah God as a sinner who needs salvation, and have you acknowledged to him that this salvation proceeds from him, the Father, through his Son Jesus Christ? (2) On the basis of this faith in God and in his provision for salvation have you dedicated yourself unreservedly to God to do his will henceforth as he reveals it to you through Jesus Christ and through the Bible under the enlightening power of the holy spirit? (*WT*, 1 August 1958, p. 478)

Further changes took place in the next fifteen years and for the first time repentance is mentioned. In addition, you are a condemned sinner unless you receive salvation.

... we suggest that you consider the following two questions, which are asked of candidates for baptism: (1) Have you repented of your sins and turned around, recognizing yourself before Jehovah God as a condemned sinner who needs salvation, and have acknowledged to him that this salvation proceeds from him, the Father, through his Son Jesus Christ? (2) On the basis of this faith in God and his provision for salvation, have you dedicated yourself unreservedly to God to do his will henceforth as he reveals it to you through Jesus Christ and through the Bible under the enlightening power of the holy spirit? (*WT*, 1 May 1973, p. 280)

Over the years not only were the questions evolving but also the fact as to whether you needed to answer questions at all.

Decision Based on Knowledge ... Before reaching this point of baptism, all candidates have carefully reviewed with congregational elders the Bible's principal doctrines and guidelines for Christian conduct to make sure they really qualify for baptism ... the baptism candidates will be in a position to answer with depth of understanding and heartfelt appreciation two simple questions ... On the basis of the sacrifice of Jesus Christ, have you repented of your sins and dedicated yourself to Jehovah to do his will? ... Do you understand that your dedicating and baptism identify you as one of Jehovah's Witnesses in association with God's spirit-directed organization? (*WT*, 1 June 1985, p. 30)

With baptism so vital to the salvation plan of a Witness it is revealing to look at the questions they are asked today compared with the ones in the past. Note that today;

- There is no mention of Jesus being your personal saviour – now it is a corporate salvation.
- There is no mention of being a condemned sinner.
- There is no mention that salvation proceeds from the Father through Jesus; it's from the organisation.
- There is no mention of the word salvation at all.
- There is no mention of dedication to do God's will but only to serve the organisation.

This shows the true basis of salvation according to the Society.

The mediator

Apart from the double-talk concerning salvation there is the serious matter of who brings salvation to the majority of Jehovah's Witnesses? Biblically of course, the mediator of our salvation is Jesus Christ but we see on p. 133 that Jesus is not the mediator of the 'great crowd.' What must they do?

> Your ATTITUDE towards the wheatlike anointed 'brothers' of Christ and the TREATMENT YOU ACCORD THEM will be THE DETERMINING FACTOR as to whether you go into 'everlasting cutting-off' or receive 'everlasting life'. (*WT*, 1 August 1981, p. 26)

> This pastoral King tells us how a person may be considered fit to be separated to the side of divine favor in contrast to the goatlike people. It is by DOING GOOD TO THOSE YET REMAINING ON EARTH OF THE SPIRITUAL 'BROTHERS' of the reigning King ... (*WT*, 1 January 1983, p. 13)

The vast majority of Jehovah's Witnesses alive today are not in the new covenant mediated by Jesus Christ, therefore Jesus Christ cannot be their mediator. However, as everyone needs a mediator, who is the mediator of the 'great crowd?' The answer from Watchtower material is the 144,000! Therefore, the 'great crowd' does not worry so much about their relationship with Jesus Christ but their relationship with the 144,000 represented by the remnant of approximately 8000 still alive on the earth today. How can the Society be God's organisation when men and women of the Society have replaced the Son of God!

What was the point of Jesus' coming?

> The next day he saw Jesus coming to him, and said, 'Behold, the Lamb of God who takes away the sin of the world!' (John 1:29, NASB)

For God so loved the world, that He gave His only begotten Son, that whoever believes in Him should not perish, but have eternal life. (John 3:16, NASB)

Jesus came for everyone that whoever ...! The Witness believes that this close relationship is for the 144,000 alone, but seek to get them to read the Bible. Ask them, 'will you be judged on your obedience to God's clearly written and understood word or on Watchtower publications?' Having establish this groundwork turn to John 3:3, 'Unless anyone is born again he cannot see the kingdom of God.' (NWT) Normally the Witness would dismiss this as being just for the 144,000 but underline that the Bible here speaks of only one Kingdom and indeed the last chapters of Revelation show this to be so. Whether they believe in a heavenly or earthly kingdom is not important here. What is important is that there is only one way into that kingdom. Also point out that their Bible says 'unless anyone'. Are you an anyone? If this is only for the 144,000 then God's word is false when it says 'anyone'.

The cross
An essential aspect of Jesus' finished work is, of course, the cross. The Witnesses seek to confuse the issue by claiming that Jesus died on a stake. When talking to a Jehovah's Witness this can often be left to one side by simply stating that it is not the shape that we should care about, but what happened on it. Even so there may be times when we need to deal with this issue and so the Additional Study starting on p. 214 will be helpful.

The Biblical testimony concerning the cross
One cannot help but notice that the series of events, regarding the death of Jesus, recorded in the gospels harmonises with the method of crucifixion described in the Additional Study. It appears that Jesus carried the cross-beam, or patibulum, to Golgotha. There, the patibulum was affixed to an upright stake,

perhaps having a seat or footpiece, and Jesus was nailed on to the whole structure. Above Him was placed the title, JESUS THE NAZARENE, THE KING OF THE JEWS.

When Jesus reappeared to His disciples in His resurrected body, He still bore the marks left by the nails in His hands. The Society teach that Jesus was a spirit at that time and just materialised a body and thereby infer that Jesus was lying. How much better to believe the Word for what it says, that it was Jesus, and His hands still had the marks of the nails.

The apostle John tells us that Thomas, who was not there when Jesus first appeared to the rest, would not believe it was actually Jesus. He told the others 'Unless I shall see in His HANDS the imprint of THE NAILS, and put my finger in the place of THE NAILS, and put my hand into His side, I will not believe.' (John 20:25, NASB)

Thomas knew there was more than one nail that punctured Jesus' hands. Yet, the Society always pictures Jesus as having one nail through both hands!

Apparently feeling that it needed to respond to this challenge, the Governing Body wrote an article for the *Questions from the Readers* in *WT*, 1 April 1984, p. 31. It clouds the issue with a partial quote from *The Cyclopaedia of Biblical, Theological, and Ecclesiastical Literature* (which does not support its claim) in an effort to make it appear as a 'waste of time' to speculate on how many nails there were. Then the article implies that Thomas was sloppy in his speech, saying that although Thomas only mentions the nail holes in his hands, he might have been referring to the nails in Jesus' feet as well. The article concludes with the statement:

> Thus, it is just not possible at this point to state with certainty how many nails were used. Any drawing of Jesus on the stake should be understood as artist's productions that offer merely a representation based on the limited facts that we have. Debate over such an insignificant detail should not be permitted to becloud the all-impor-

tant truth that 'we became reconciled to God through the death of his Son'. (Rom. 5:10)

It appears that since the evidence has swung against the Society in this manner, it is resorting to the old technique of accusing the opposition of what it is in fact guilty of. The Society is the group that is accusing others of 'false worship' by using the symbol of the cross. As far as Christians are concerned, the exact method of crucifixion is not a big issue. Rather, the manner in which the Bible presents the cross is the real issue.

Paul's testimony concerning the cross

Jews viewed execution by the cross as an accursed way to die. Similarly, the Watchtower views the concept of Christ dying on a stake in a negative light. See for instance, *Aw.*, 8 November 1972, p. 27, which denounces those who worship the cross. There is no justification for worshipping before the cross or kissing it; but there is justification for considering the cross as a symbol of Christianity. The Jews may have considered the cross a shameful thing, but the apostle Paul boasted of the cross of Christ. (Gal. 6:14)

The first chapter of 1 Cor. 1:17-18 tells us that Christ sent Paul to preach the message of the cross. He knew some (like the Jews and Jehovah's Witnesses?) would stumble over the cross, others would consider it foolishness but to Christians the cross would mean the power and wisdom of God! God deliberately chose the weak, foolish and despised things of the world to make His point.

This has been the message of the church throughout the centuries – Jesus died on the cross for our sins. He is now alive and can live through us (1 Cor. 15:1-3; Luke 24:45-47). This message can only be understood with God's spirit and so groups using intellectual persuasion and material hopes as their main emphasis miss the true meaning.

Paul also uses the cross as a symbol for the cause of Christianity, as well as the death of the old nature. See Phil.

3:18, Col. 2:14, Gal. 2:20; 5:24. Over and over Paul considers the cross a sign of victory, not defeat! He boasted in the cross!

Christians are not afraid of the cross nor do they worship it. It is simply a symbol representing the greatest act of love in the universe!

Summary

First, the Society's arguments concerning the Greek words *stauros* and *xylon* offer no proof for its point.

Second, whatever usage of the cross existed before or after the time of Christ is irrelevant to the issue, as there is no conclusive evidence that first-century Jews or Christians looked upon the crucifixion as a specifically pagan symbol. It was a means to an end – the punishment or death of a criminal. Symbols mean different things at different times. At any rate, Jesus did not choose the instrument of death. In addition, the cross appears in excavations much earlier than the Watchtower's claim of fourth century AD.

Third, archaeological evidence, if anything, proves Jesus died on the traditional cross. There is little or no contention on this point among modern scholars.

Fourth, while Jews of Paul's day may not have used visual symbols due to their extreme view of pictorial representations, the cross nevertheless became the symbol of the Christian faith. Though objects or symbols are not to be worshipped, the apostle Paul gloried in the cross as the Christian sign of victory!

Finally, we would want to reiterate that the most vital thing is not the shape of the instrument on which Jesus died but what happened on it. Some Witnesses will be genuinely interested in the archaeological finds, others will seek to use the 'stake' issue as an evasive tactic. Whichever it is, seek to share the glorious sacrifice of Jesus and what it means for us today, that He became sin and died.

9

The Afterlife

Resurrection is the proof of our salvation. It is not just that Christ died but that He rose again. Resurrection is therefore a vital part of a Christian's life.

The Watchtower's definition of resurrection is summed up on p. 333 of *Reasoning*:

> (It) literally means 'a standing up again' and it refers to a rising up from death ... Resurrection involves a reactivating of the life pattern of the individual, which life pattern God has retained in his memory. According to God's will for the individual, the person is restored in either a human or a spirit body and yet retains his personal identity, having the same personality and memory as when he died.

In the pages that follow this description, not one Scripture is put forward to support the view. We will check the definition against the Scriptures.

Resurrection is not the most correct term for what the Society teaches, it is more akin to re-creation. An interesting quote appeared in *WT*, from the archbishop of the Greek Orthodox Church of North and South America.

> Paul's conception of the resurrection body has nothing to do with the resuscitation of dead bodies from the grave ... His conception of resurrection body may be

better expressed as transformation, RECREATION, AND RECONSTITUTION, by the power of God, of the whole man's unity ... (*WT*, 15 May 1992, p. 9)

Christ's resurrection

What happened to Jesus in His resurrection will in measure happen to us. Did God the Father remember the life pattern of Jesus and bring Him back with the same 'personal identity, having the same personality?' If He did, it appears from Luke 24:13ff, John 20:15, etc. that something went wrong because people did not recognise Him. The Watchtower explains this by saying Jesus materialised different bodies, but this would be deception. There are other verses that have to be explained too, for instance John 10:17-18:

> ... I lay down My life that I may take it again. No one has taken it away from Me, but I lay it down on My own initiative. I have authority to lay it down, and I have authority to take it up again. This commandment I received from My Father. (NASB)

Jesus had authority to take up his own life again. If every part of Jesus died why did the Father give Him a commandment to take up His own life? Added to this is John 2:19-21 where again Jesus said 'I will raise up My body'. Did Jesus tell lies? Of course not! He was both showing His clear authority as God and that there is part of man that is eternal.

Summarising pp. 334-35 of *Reasoning* we read that Jesus only materialised bodies and therefore did not have His own resurrection body. He was resurrected a spirit as 1 Pet. 3:18 and 1 Cor. 15:45 clearly show. This is despite the fact that He said in Luke 24:36-39, 'a spirit does not have flesh and bones as you see that I have.'

Do the, phrases, 'made alive in the spirit' of 1 Pet. 3:18 and, 'life-giving spirit' of 1 Cor. 15:45 mean, as the Watchtower claims, that Jesus was raised a spirit creature? The resurrection life of Christ was obviously a 'spiritual life,' no longer with the confines of the human body. But how does Scripture describe this life?

> So also is the resurrection of the dead. It is sown a perishable body, it is raised an imperishable body; it is sown in dishonour, it is raised in glory; it is sown in weakness, it is raised in power; it is sown a natural body, it is raised a spiritual body. If there is a natural body, there is also a spiritual body. So also it is written, 'The first man, Adam became a living soul.' The last Adam became a life-giving spirit. (1 Cor. 15:42-45, NASB)

The context of 1 Cor. 15 is the body becoming imperishable and immortal. Greek scholar W. E. Vine comments on the Greek word *soma*, which is translated 'body' in the above Scriptures

> The body is an essential part of the man and therefore the redeemed are not perfected till the resurrection, Heb 11:40; no man in his final state will be without his body, John 5:28-29; Rev. 20:13. (*Vine*, Vol. 1, p. 136-37)

Scripture uses 'body' in the sense that at the resurrection we will have spiritual bodies. Just as we have had bodies suitable for this earth, so we will have bodies suitable for our new spiritual life. Jesus was not raised a spirit creature but with a new spiritual body that did not have the limitations of His old earthly one. Scripture also describes Christians with 'bodies' now as 'in the spirit' (see Rom. 8:8-9), therefore there is no problem with the use of a similar term in 1 Pet. for Christ with a resurrection body.

Our resurrection
Rev. 20:4 shows the 'firstfruits' in the resurrection are those who have gone through the tribulation without worshipping

the beast. Verses 12 and 13 then make it clear that all others, good or bad, will receive a resurrection, not just those whom God remembers. The division is then made at the judgement between those who receive eternal life and those who receive eternal death.

Reasoning, pp. 338-39 seeks to prove that the rest of the dead not coming to life until after the thousand years refers to more than their resurrection. This allows them to say they are resurrected during the thousand years but only come to life, that is, attain human perfection, after the thousand years. However, the word used here in Rev. 20:4 is the same as the one used in Rom. 14:9 of Christ's resurrection which is complete and full already.

The Society also claims that no one resurrected is to be consigned to a second death. The explanation in *Reasoning*, p. 338, is a classic piece of Watchtower contortionism:

> What is the meaning of John 5:28,29? ... What Jesus said here must be understood in the light of the later revelation that he gave to John. (See Revelation 20:12-13..) Both those who formerly did good things and those who formerly practised bad things will be 'judged individually according to their deeds'. What deeds? If we were to take the view that people were going to be condemned on the basis of deeds in their past life, that would be inconsistent with Romans 6:7: 'He who has died has been acquitted from his sin.' IT WOULD ALSO BE UNREASONABLE to resurrect people simply for them to be destroyed. So, at John 5:28-29a, Jesus was pointing ahead to the resurrection; then, in the remainder of verse 29, he was expressing the outcome after they had been uplifted to human perfection and been put on judgement.

The Scripture says, but we do not believe it therefore we will change it. The Scriptures in John 5 and in Rev. 20 clearly show that the judgement comes after the resurrection and is based on what is already written within the books. Bringing in Rom. 6 is simply a peg on which to hang an illogical conclusion because the context of Rom. 6 is not physical death but spiritual death in Christ.

The resurrection to life depends on knowing Jesus in our hearts now, before we die, and it is because of Him that we have authority to 'take up our lives again.' Unless we have had our sins cleansed by the precious blood of Jesus and our names written in the Lamb's Book of Life there is no resurrection to life. Nowhere in the Bible do we find the doctrine of the second chance.

1 Cor. 15:20 tells us that Christ's resurrection is the firstfruit, there are more to come of the same kind. Then in verses 42 onwards we read that the body that is sown is raised again a different body. Instead of being a perishable, weak, natural body, it will be an imperishable, powerful, spiritual body. Verses 50 onwards show that resurrection is not just an important coming back to where we left off, hoping for better things, but a powerful, mighty tool of God that swallows up the last enemy, death.

Soul, death and hell

The Watchtower teaching about the soul is 'In the Bible, "soul" is translated from the Hebrew *nephesh* and the Greek *psykhe*. Bible usage shows the soul to be a person or an animal or the life that a person or an animal enjoys.' (*Reasoning*, p. 375)

> ... the Scriptures show that both *psykhe* and *nephesh*, as used with reference to earthly creatures, refer to that which is material, tangible, visible and morta l... the Scriptures clearly show that *nephesh* and *psykhe* are used to designate the animal creation ... Man was distinct from the animal creation, but that distinction was not because he was a *nephesh* ('soul') and they were not ... So, too, the 'spirit' (Heb[rew] *ruach*; Gr[eek] *pneuma*) or

life force of man is not distinct from the life force in animals. (*Insight*, Vol. 2, pp. 1004/5)

The Witnesses conclude that there is no immortality of the soul, no consciousness after death. To find the truth we must be acquainted with the Greek and Hebrew words.

The Hebrew word *nephesh* literally means 'a breathing' creature but is used widely. *Psykhe* is the Greek word denoting the breath, the breath of life, then the soul in all its meanings. The literal meaning of the Hebrew word *ruach* is 'wind' and, by resemblance, 'breath'. Primarily the Greek word *pneuma* denotes the wind, but also breath and then especially the spirit which like the wind is invisible, immaterial and powerful.

The *Reasoning* article on the soul begins on p. 375 with the question 'What does the Bible say that helps us to understand what the soul is?'

The Society says that the word can mean the person or the life of the person, and takes no account of the other different meanings that every biblical Greek and Hebrew scholar is aware of. It concludes from Josh. 11:11 that the soul cannot be the part of man that survives death because it is struck by the sword. However, the word *nephesh* is used here as the person and so no evidence about the inward man can be gleaned. Is it possible, however, to use the Society's definition of soul, 'a person or an animal or the life that a person or an animal enjoys' in all 754 times *nephesh* appears. Check the following Scriptures.

- Lev. 17:11- If my soul is no different to that of an animal why make blood atonement for the soul?
- 2 Sam. 11:11 – Is Uriah repeating himself? Surely, he is showing that the soul is more than just life.
- Is. 42:1 – God who is a spirit has a soul which obviously transcends animal or human life.
- Ps. 42:1-2 – This is not the natural life of a man. As the psalmist says in verse 7, 'deep calls to deep'.

We must also comment on the Society's misunderstanding of Gen. 2:7.

> Man was thus made up of only two independent elements, the corporeal and the spiritual: but when God placed the spirit within the casing of the earth, the combination of these produced a third part, and man became a living soul. Direct communication between spirit and flesh is impossible: their intercourse can be carried on only by means of a medium, and the instant production of one was the result of their contact in Adam. He became a living soul in the sense that spirit and body were completely merged in this third part. (E. H. Bancroft, *Christian Theology*, 1980, pp. 187-88)

What we see is that Adam was complete as a person but was not called a *nephesh*, soul. Then 'life' was placed in him by means of God's breath. That life was not *nephesh* but it made him a nephesh. In other words in this verse neither 'a person' nor 'the life of a person' defines *nephesh*.

The New Testament also has problems of definition for the Jehovah's Witnesses.

Mark 8:35 – It's nonsense if we say whoever loses himself or the life within him... shall save it. The only way you can lose your life is to die and that in itself does not save you. Jesus was saying that we are to lose our soul, our immortal part, to Him.

Matt. 10:28 – The Watchtower's argument on this verse is basically that men can kill the body but not the person for all time and because God can destroy the soul it is not immortal or indestructible. The Bible teaches that no one on earth can destroy the soul, it is immortal. The fact that the immortal eternal God can destroy it does not mean that it is not indestructible or immortal, God can do anything! In addition, the fact that God can destroy the soul, in the after life proves that there is immortal life going beyond death.

John 10:17-18 – The Society says that once Jesus laid down

His soul it was gone, therefore He could not take it up again. But Jesus says He has authority over His soul before and after death.

Rev. 6:9; 20:4 – A dead person cannot be a soul!

3 John 2 – A distinction is made between the good health of the life and the welfare of the soul.

The Scriptures reveal that the Watchtower's definition of soul is not God's definition. The Bible often uses it just to describe the person, but in its fuller sense, it describes that part which was formed to enable flesh and spirit to communicate. It is the deep invisible and immortal part of the man, which at death leaves the body and returns to God. It does not cease to exist, because God alone has power over the destiny of the soul and He has given it immortality.

Man and animals have a nephesh

The Society points out that both man and animals are called by the same term, *nephesh*, and that is illogical. *Reasoning* asks 'Do other scholars who are not Jehovah's Witnesses acknowledge that this is what the Bible says the soul is?' (*Reasoning*, p. 377)

Scholars are quoted as 'proof' of their agreement and as usual, what the Society has missed out is supplied in bold

> There is no dichotomy [division] of body and soul in the O[ld] T[estament]. The Israelite saw things concretely, in their totality, and thus he considered men as persons and not as composites. The term '*nepes*' [*ne'phesh*], though translated by our word soul, never means soul as distinct from the body or the individual person ... **At death the '*nepes*' goes to Sheol, a place of insensitive, shadowy existence. Many psalms pray for the rescue of one's '*nepes*' from death, where the rescue means to be saved from dying, not to be raised from the dead** ... The term [*psykhe*] is the N[ew] T[estament] word corresponding with '*nepes*'. It can mean the principle of life,

life itself, or the living being. **Through Hellenistic influence, unlike *'nepes'*, it was opposed to body and considered immortal. The *psyche* in Matthew 10:28 ... means a life that exits separately from the body.** (*NCE*, Vol. XIII, 1967, pp. 449-50)

The Hebrew term for 'soul' (*'nefesh'*, that which breathes) was used by Moses ... signifying an 'animated being' and applicable equally to non-human beings. **The Hebrews used the term to apply to the entire personality but reserved the concept *'ruach'* ('spirit') to denote a principle of life, mind', and occasionally 'heart'. *'Nefesh'* was often used as if it were the seat of appetite, emotion, and passion and, conjoined with 'heart', was held to encompass intellect, will, and feeling.** New Testament usage of *'psyche'* ('soul') was comparable to *'nefesh'*. (*EB, Macropaedia*, Vol. 15, 1976, p. 152)

The belief that the soul continues its existence after the dissolution of the body is a matter of philosophical or theological speculation rather than of simple faith, and is accordingly nowhere expressly taught in Holy Scripture ... **It is the Psalmist's implicit faith in God's omnipotence and omnipresence that leads him to the hope of immortality.** (*The Jewish Encyclopaedia* Vol. VI, 1910, p. 564)

The *Reasoning* article continues with the question, 'Is the soul the same as the spirit?' (p. 378). In a brief outline such as this, it is not possible to answer this question in depth. However, the Scriptures do show that the soul and the spirit are separate but also linked. (see 1 Thess. 5:23 and Heb. 4:12)

The Society makes much of Eccles. 12:7 but it misses the whole point. The dust is said to 'return' to the earth, that is, the body goes back to the place it came from. Therefore the point being made about the spirit is that it too 'returns' (same Hebrew word) to where it came from, God.

Using this verse and Eccles. 3:19-22 as the Society does shows ignorance for the revelation of the whole of God's Word and especially of the Book of Ecclesiastes. Ecclesiastes is in the 'Wisdom' section of the Old Testament and as such shows us how to live, not what to believe. There are two speakers in the book, the humanist in chapters 1-11, apart from two brief passages, and the theist (speaking for God) in chapter 12. What is recorded in chapter 3 is from the humanist, and therefore it is man's opinion, not God's.

Another question *Reasoning* poses is 'What is the origin of Christendom's belief in an immortal soul?' (*Reasoning*, p. 379) Through misleading editing and much ignored evidence we are lead to believe that immortality of the soul is nothing but a product of Greek mythology and was not taught or believed in the early church.

> The Christian concept of a spiritual soul created by God and infused into the body at conception to make man a living whole is the fruit of a long development in Christian philosophy. Only with Origen (died c. 254 CE) in the East and St. Augustine (died 430 CE) in the West was the soul established as a spiritual substance and a philosophical concept formed of its nature ... **The early Fathers were not directly concerned with the nature of the human soul, although they could not avoid treating this question at least implicitly when discussing the soul's immortality ... The apologist Athenagoras (c.177) ... (taught that) a clear emphasis on the Christian view of man as a unit, a living whole, even if the immortal soul is the more important element** ... His [Augustine's] doctrine ... owed much (including some shortcomings) to Neoplatonism, **yet was much more strikingly Christian in approach and content ... (he taught that) the soul is a com-**

pletely immaterial substance ... God is the creator and maker of every soul and that the soul is not an emanation from the divine substance but a creature made to God's image. (*NCE*, Vol. XIII, 1967, pp. 452, 454) (Two pages of contrary evidence are omitted from the quote, we have only included a fraction of it.)

The problem of immortality, we have seen, engaged the serious attention of the Babylonian theologians. **While the solutions they had to offer could hardly have been satisfactory either to themselves or to the masses, it must not be supposed that the denial of immortality to man involved the total extinction of conscious vitality.** Neither the people nor the leaders of religious thought ever faced the possibility of the total annihilation of what once was called into existence. Death was a passage to another kind of life **and the denial of immortality merely emphasized the impossibility of escaping the change in existence brought about by death.** (M. Jastrow, Jr., *The Religion of Babylonia and Assyria*, Boston, 1898, p. 556)

We have already shown that Scripture teaches the immortality of the soul, but what about the early church?

The following quotes out of many show that the early church did believe it. The first quote is by Justin Martyr who, interestingly, the Society quotes as a reliable authority. (see *WT*, 15 January 1974, pp. 47-48)

For reflect upon the end of each of the preceding kings, how they died the death common to all, which if it is issued in insensibility it would be a godsend to all the wicked. But since sensation remains to all who have ever lived, and eternal punishment is laid up ... see that ye neglect not to be convinced and to hold as your belief that these things are true ... even after death souls are in a state of sensation (*Ante-Nicene Christian Library*, Vol. 2, First *Apology* of Justin Martyr [approx. AD 150], p. 22)

... the purpose of Him who fashioned us according to which he made man of an immortal soul and a body ... it is quite clear that the resurrection is plainly proved. (*Ante-Nicene Christian Library*, Vol. 2, Athenagoras on *The Resurrection of the Dead* [approx. AD 177], pp. 439-40)

The Lord has taught ... that souls not only continue to exist ... but that they preserve the same form ... When God therefore bestows life and perpetual duration, it comes to pass that even souls which did not previously exist should henceforth endure [for ever), since God has both willed that they should exist, and should continue in existence. (*Ante-Nicene Christian Library*, Vol. 5, Irenaeus *Against Heresies* [approx. AD 180], pp. 250, 251, 253)

Definition of death

The Society says death is 'The ceasing of all functions of life. After breathing, heartbeat, and brain activity stop, the life-force gradually ceases to function in body cells. Death is the opposite of life.' (*Reasoning*, p. 98)

Does this definition match up with the scriptural definition? Luke 9:60 would read that those whose life force had stopped functioning would bury those whose life force had stopped functioning. Eph. 2:1, how can we 'stop breathing in our trespasses and sins?'

Whereas *Reasoning* does not mention these verses here, *Insight* does, and it makes this revealing comment:

The death state is used to illustrate the SPIRITUALLY DEAD CONDITION ... (Luke 9:60... Eph. 2:1) ... a Christian's being freed or liberated from sin ... is also likened to death ... The one figuratively dying in such a way, of course, IS STILL ALIVE PHYSICALLY. (*Insight*, Vol. 1, p. 599)

The Society admits that Scripture uses death in a way which does not mean annihilation. If the meaning of death is non-existence then figuratively, it would mean that the Christian becomes non-existent to sin, which is not true. If death means a continuation in a different state, then the example is perfect! To understand this look at 1 Kgs. 17:22 where the widow's son was raised from the dead. 'Finally Jehovah listened to Elijah's voice, so that the soul of the child came back within him and he came to life.' (*NWT*) The soul had lived on somewhere in a different state and returning to the body caused the boy to live again.

Separated
The first occurrence of the word 'death' in Scripture is Gen. 2:17. This verse explains the punishment if man should take of the tree of good and evil, '... in the DAY you eat from it you will positively die.' (*NWT*)

Adam's physical death was many years later but what happened on the day he ate? Gen. 3:24 shows Adam and Eve were put out of the garden, that is, they were separated from God. The Bible's definition of death is separation from God. When you read Luke 9:60 and Eph. 2:1 again with this definition they make sense.

Ezek. 18:4 is often used by a Jehovah's Witness to 'prove' that the 'soul' dies and nothing lives on. However, go through the rest of Ezek. 18 and look at verses 9, 17, 19, 21, 22, 23 and especially 27. This would read, using the Watchtower definition of death, '... he is the one who will preserve his own person or the life of his person alive, he will remain in the state opposite to death.'

Dead or alive-communication!
This is another problem area for Witnesses. There are several Scriptures showing that in either death or life we have direct communication with God.

Phil. 1:20-24: Christ would be magnified in Paul's death;

death would be gain for him; leaving the earth would mean being with Christ.

2 Cor. 5:1-10: When the body is dissolved we are to have an everlasting 'house' in the heavens. While in the body we are absent from the Lord and when absent from the body we are home with the Lord! Death to Paul was an immediate release from the confines of his body and a being instantly with the Lord.

1 Thess. 5:10: Even the *NWT* is self-explanatory 'He died for us, that, whether we STAY AWAKE or ARE ASLEEP, we should LIVE TOGETHER with him.'

Hell

The Watchtower's teaching is explained on pp. 168-75 of *Reasoning*:

> The Hebrew [word] *sheol* and its Greek equivalent *hades*, which refer, not to an individual burial place, but to the common grave of dead mankind; also the Greek [word] *gehenna* which is used as a symbol of eternal destruction. (p. 169)

Emphasis is given on p. 175 to the fact that the Babylonians and other heathen empires believed in hell. This is simply a smoke screen, as the only evidence that matters is what the Bible teaches. The article concludes by saying that the concept of hell comes from the Devil, not from God.

With their belief, the Jehovah's Witnesses can 'prove' that hell is not a literal place and that when a man is dead he is unconscious and unaware of what is happening. First, we will look at the words translated 'hell', 'grave', etc., in some Scripture passages in the *NWT*, and see if the translation fits the context.

Hebrew word sheol

Can this refer to the common grave of mankind? If so there can be no eternal spirit and we would be just a memory in the mind of God waiting to be remembered and restored. However, this definition gives problems with the following Scriptures, amongst others, in the *NWT*.

'Even Sheol underneath has become agitated ... At you it has awakened those impotent in death ... All of them speak up and say...' (Is. 14:9-10, *NWT*) How can they speak?

'... the distressing circumstances of Sheol themselves found me.' (Ps. 116:3, *NWT*) What are the distressing circumstances?

'... that you may deliver his very soul from Sheol itself.' (Prov. 23:14, *NWT*) It is possible not to go to Sheol!

'... Let them go down into Sheol alive ...' (Ps. 55:15, *NWT*). You can get there and still be alive!

'This is the way of those who have stupidity ... they have been appointed to Sheol itself ... God himself will redeem my soul from the hand of Sheol, for he will receive me' (Ps. 49:13-15, *NWT*). The psalmist saw a distinct difference between himself and the stupid with relation to sheol.

Greek word hades

'... and the gates of Hades shall not overpower it' (Matt. 16:18, *NWT*). If hades were the place of the unconscious, it would be understood that it could not overpower the church.

'And in Hades he lifted up his eyes ... cried out and said ...' (Luke 16:23-24, *NWT*). The Society wants to dismiss this as a parable but even so it must be a true story and therefore the rich man was alive in hades.

'... and death and Hades gave up those dead in them, and they were judged ...' (Rev. 20:13, *NWT*). From hades the only resurrection is to judgement, not to live for a thousand years.

Greek word gehenna

'... it is finer [better] for you to enter into life maimed than with two hands to go off into Gehenna, into the fire that cannot be put out.' (Mark 9:43, *NWT*) Being maimed in this life is a serious matter; how would it be better to go into unconsciousness?

Notice also the 'everlasting' quality, a fire that cannot be put out. This is seen in other Scriptures. Matt. 25:46 is one example that the Witnesses try to get around by giving a secondary meaning to the word 'punishment'. But this verse contrasts the righteous going into 'eternal life', a life that will last for ever, with the wicked going into eternal 'cutting-off' (*NWT*). There is nothing eternal about being annihilated.

Greek word paradeisos

The Society makes much of Luke 23:43 (see *Reasoning*, pp. 286-87). It cannot believe the eternal soul of the thief could continue in part of heaven or hades so it relegates it to 'resurrection' on earth at some time in the future. What is the evidence concerning the Greek word?

> *Paradeisos* ... In Luke 23:43, the promise of the Lord to the repentant robber was FULFILLED THE SAME DAY; Christ, at His death, having committed His spirit to the Father, went in spirit IMMEDIATELY INTO HEAVEN itself, THE DWELLING PLACE OF GOD. (*Vine*, Vol. 3, p. 158)

Reasoning rightly says that J. B. Rotherham's *Emphasized Bible* agrees with its way of punctuating the verse, 'I say to you today, ...' But it doesn't tell you that as a footnote it shows, 'I say to you, Today ...' as a correct alternative.

Summary

Scriptures do not agree with the definitions given to the three words by the Society, rather they show that *sheol* and *hades* are the place of waiting after death. The part of man that is eternal is 'alive' there during this time. *Gehenna* is the final place of everlasting punishment to which the wicked are banished after judgement.

Judgement

The Society sums up the time of judgement as follows:

> These 144,000 joint heirs of Jesus Christ, instead of being judged, will sit with him on thrones of judgement... There was a previous judgement period for these 144,000 when they were on earth ... For redeemed mankind in general to have a time of judgement here on earth there needs to be a resurrection ... Jesus said ... that the 'hour' would come ... during the 1,000-year reign of Jesus Christ with his 144,000 glorified joint heirs ... Of course, during their sleep of death there comes no change in their personality. (*WT*, 1 September 1978, pp. 21-22)

What does the Bible teach?

Heb. 9:27: 'We die once and then comes judgement.' There is not one Scripture that teaches that anyone will be raised again during the thousand years and be given a second chance.

Rev. 20:1-15: These verses show the events of the judgement.

- Verse 1. This is the beginning of the thousand years
- Verse 4. According to the Society, those on the thrones are the 144,000
- Verse 5. Therefore, they are alone during the thousand years, because the rest of the dead do not come alive until after the thousand years are complete
- Verse 7. End of the thousand years
- Verse 12. Now the dead are judged
- Verse 13. They are judged individually according to their deeds, not because they belong to the WBTS
- Verse 15. The basis of judgement is whether my name was written in the Lamb's Book of Life when I died. It cannot be written there after I died. There is no second chance.

The kingdom

This is another aspect of the afterlife to the Watchtower. *Reasoning* sums up the teaching.

> The Kingdom of God is the expression of Jehovah's universal sovereignty toward his creatures, or the means used by him to express that sovereignty. The term is used particularly to designate the manifestation of God's sovereignty through the royal government headed by his Son, Jesus Christ. 'Kingdom' may refer to the rulership of the one anointed as King or to the earthly realm ruled by that heavenly government. (pp. 225-26)

The article continues by commenting on Luke 17:21 and that, as Jesus was speaking to the Pharisees, He could not possibly mean that, 'the Kingdom was in their hearts. But the Kingdom as presented by Christ was in their midst'. (p. 226)

The summary of the teaching is that the kingdom will be a literal one, ruled over by Jesus and the 144,000, and that it began in 1914.

What does the Bible teach?

Heb. 12:28 in the literal Greek shows that we receive the kingdom now!

Luke 17:21, Matt. 3:2 and 12:28 all show that the kingdom exists wherever the King is manifested and accepted in His rightful position.

Luke 12:32, we are told by the Society, is the heavenly kingdom being received by the 144,000. But the same Greek word, *basileia*, is used in Matt. 25:34 where we are told the earthly ones are receiving their 'kingdom'. The Greek makes no distinction between the heavenly kingdom and the earthly kingdom.

Rev. 21:24 shows that the kings of the earth will bring their glory into the 'capital city' of the heavenly kingdom. How can that be if the two kingdoms are completely separate?

The Bible teaches that there will be no great gulf between

two kingdoms. It shows a new heavens and a new earth but undivided, mingled together as it was in the beginning.

Luke 13:28 and *Matt. 8:11* show Abraham, Isaac and Jacob in the heavenly kingdom, but *Matt. 8:12* shows the sons of the kingdom thrown out!

The Greek word for 'kingdom' is always *basileia* which, according to Greek scholar W. E. Vine,

> is primarily an abstract noun, DENOTING SOVEREIGNTY, royal power, dominion... then, by metonymy [using an attribute of something as its name, e.g. 'Crown' for 'king'], a concrete noun, denoting the territory, or people over whom a king rules.' (*Vine*, Vol. 2, p. 294)

A more literal rendering of the Greek is 'kingship,' that is, the kingdom is only in existence because the King is ruling. No King, no kingdom. The word has much more to do with the act of ruling than the literal territory of the kingdom.

The Scriptures teach that the kingdom mainly affects us in a spiritual way now and the completeness of the literal kingdom will only take place when Christ returns to this earth. The Watchtower has placed an over emphasis on this literal expression and practically ignores the spiritual effect on our lives today.

The new heavens and the new earth

This is the final aspect of the Watchtower after life that we need to look at.

Reasoning, p. 113, asks the question, 'Will God himself destroy the earth by fire?' In answer it quotes two Scriptures: 2 Pet. 3:7,10 and Rev. 21:1, from the King James version. It then argues that we must take these verses in context and discover that it is not a literal burning up but a symbolic one.

> It is that symbolic 'earth', or wicked human society, that is 'discovered'; that is Jehovah will sear away as by fire all

disguise, exposing the wickedness of ungodly human society and showing it to be worthy of complete destruction. That wicked society of humans is also 'the first earth', referred to at Revelation 21:1. (*Reasoning*, p. 115)

This teaching is amplified in *WT*, 1 November 1974, pp. 665-667 and can be summarised as follows:

1. The story of Noah is a prophetic picture. Noah = Jesus Christ. Noah's wife = the remnant of the Bride of Christ still on earth. The sons and their wives = the great crowd. The ark = spiritual paradise into which God has brought worshippers.
2. The fire that is coming is not all literal, although part of it may be. The earth will be cleansed and become a perfect place to live.
3. 'Heavens' and 'earth' are not literal, but represent 'systems of governments.'
4. The fulfilment of this 'prophecy' began in 1919.
5. The ark = spiritual paradise = Jehovah's Witness congregations.

What does the Bible teach?
2 Pet. 3:1-13 compares the judgement of Noah's flood with the judgement of fire in the last days.

• Verse 5 shows a literal heavens and earth existed in the past
• Verse 7 shows a literal heavens and earth exist now
• Verse 6 shows that literal water was used as a judgement
• Verse 7 shows that literal fire will be used as a judgement
• Verse 6 shows that everything in the world (*kosmos*) was destroyed
• Verse 7 shows ungodly men will be destroyed
• Verse 10 shows that the heavens and earth will be burned up

Everything was literal at the flood and everything will be literal in the last days. The Greek words used for heaven, *ouranos*, and earth, *ge*, are used in Scripture for the literal earth and the literal heavens. There is nothing here to suggest that the words should be spiritualised as a 'system'. There are three sets of 'heaven and earth' mentioned and each set is literal.

- Verse 5. The original ones created by the Lord
- Verse 7. The present ones instituted after the flood
- Verse 13. The new ones yet to come

The heavens will pass away and the elements will be destroyed. The earth, with its entire works, will be burned up. As with the flood, all the inhabitants are to be destroyed unless they are in the 'ark' of the New Testament.

The Greek word for 'new' used in these verses is *kainos* which has the meaning of 'new in quality not time' and of 'a different nature from of old'. The very heavens and earth will undergo a change, which could never be brought about by a thousand years of work by all the Jehovah's Witnesses. It is an essential change of character that only the miraculous working of God can produce.

To the Jehovah's Witness the 'ark' pictures 'the spiritual paradise into which God has brought his worshipers today.' But the ark only enabled Noah and his family to ride out God's judgement, it was a temporary dwelling place. 1 Pet. 3:20 shows the ark as the means of salvation, not a place of long residence. The worst part of this typology is that the Society's 'ark' is being a baptised member of the WBTS and actively associating with the local congregation. This is blasphemy because the WBTS has placed itself in place of Jesus Christ. 1 Pet. 3:18-22 shows Jesus Christ is the Ark that will bring us safe through God's judgement into eternal life.

Part of this typology actually destroys the Society's belief. According to it Noah's wife, representing the remnant of the 144,000, and the sons and daughters, representing the 'great crowd', were all in the same ark and all went to the same place! Without realising it, it has stumbled on the truth. All who are in the true 'ark' are brought to one place! There is not a two-tier salvation.

10

Eternal Life

_ ୶ _

At the end of this age, when the Society believes that Armageddon, God's final battle strikes, people will be divided into three classes. Only loyal active Jehovah's Witnesses will survive and so the majority alive at that time will become part of the third group mentioned below.

1. The 144,000 or 'little flock' who will reign with Jesus in heaven. Those of their number who have already died received an immediate resurrection into heaven.
2. The Great Crowd or 'other sheep' who are worthy of a resurrection will come to life and live on paradise earth. The majority of people will receive such a resurrection and a second chance but they could still be annihilated if they are disobedient.
3. Those not worthy of a resurrection or those destroyed at Armageddon will be annihilated and have no future at all.

The 144,000

A summary of the Society's teaching on the 144,000 is that Luke 12:32 shows only a 'little flock' inheriting the kingdom. Rev. 7:1-8 and 14:1-5 show this 'little flock' to number 144,000 and Rev. 5:9-10 further shows they will rule as 'kings and priests'.

The 144,000 are in direct contrast to the 'great crowd' which does not have a heavenly future but an earthly one. According to the Society, John 10:16 shows that this earthly group is called 'other sheep' or 'great crowd' (Rev. 7:9-17). During the millennium, when the earth is a paradise, all those counted worthy of a resurrection (John 5:28-29) will have an opportunity to learn obedience and loyalty to the organisational structures that God establishes through the 144,000 and Jesus Christ reigning in heaven (Rev. 20:11-15).

Is this scriptural?

> Those who are called by God to share in such heavenly service are few in number. As Jesus said, they are a 'little flock'. Years after his return to heaven, Jesus made known the exact number in a vision to the apostle John, who wrote: 'I saw, and, look! the Lamb standing upon Mount Zion, and with him a hundred and forty-four thousand ... who have been bought from the earth'. (*The Truth that Leads to Eternal Life*, WBTS, 1968, p. 77; see also *Reasoning* p. 166)

The Society claims a scriptural link between the 'little flock' and the 144,000, but is there one? The 'little flock' promise was made to the apostles, literal Israel, but the 144,000 are, according to Watchtower teaching, spiritual Israel. In any case, the 'little flock' of verse 32 is a comparison with the thousands of verse 1. No link there.

In John 10:16 the Jews listening to Jesus were told that there were 'other sheep' who would be brought into 'one flock with one shepherd.' Eph. 2:11-16 explains that the 'other sheep' are Gentiles who would become 'one body' with Jews through Jesus. There is no link here because there is no place for two distinct groups.

> '144,000 redeemed from Earth to be Kings and Priests with Christ in Heaven ... Rev 14:1,4 ... Rev 5:9-10' (*Make Sure Of All Things*, 1965, p. 303).

The Bible does not link these two Scriptures as being the same people. In fact, the 144,000 are shown to be different from the people in Rev. 5.

Rev. 7:4 – '... from every tribe of the sons of Israel' (NASB)

Rev. 5:9 – '... from every tribe and tongue and people and nation' (NASB)

Those in Rev. 5 are not the 144,000 but they are a kingdom of priests to God. Moreover, the Scripture shows they are the great crowd! '... from every nation and all tribes and peoples and tongues.' (Rev. 7:9, NASB)

> Revelation does not say of them [the great crowd] as it does of the 144,000, that they are 'bought from the earth'... The description of them as 'standing before the throne and before the Lamb' indicates not necessarily a location, but an approved condition ... The expression ... [means] literally, 'in sight of the throne'. (*Reasoning,* p. 167)

First, when we compare Rev. 5:9 with 7:9 as we did above, we do find that the great crowd are 'bought.' We will also note that Rev. 7:1-4 shows that the 144,000 are 'on the EARTH.'

Secondly, the phrase 'in sight of the throne' (Greek, *enopion tou thronou*) is a unique description used by the apostle John, only in Revelation, and seven out of the nine times it appears (referring to the seven lamps, the glassy sea, the golden altar, the seven spirits, the twenty-four elders, the angels, the four living creatures and the 144,000) Jehovah's Witnesses are convinced that it means being literally 'in the temple of God where the heavenly throne is.' The remaining two occurrences, where the 'great crowd' are before God's throne, are said to be not literal.

The phrase 'before the throne'
Thirdly, there is another phrase, other than 'before the throne', used of the great crowd. Rev. 7:15 shows them to be 'in His

temple,' the divine habitation. The Greek word is *naos* about which Greek scholar W. E. Vine says;

> ... a shrine or sanctuary ... into which only the priests could lawfully enter, e.g., Luke 1:9,21,22; Christ, as being of the tribe of Judah, and thus not being a priest while upon earth ... did not enter the *naos*. (*Vine*, Vol. 4, p. 115)

The great crowd must be where the Lord is, not just in an approved condition. Indeed Rev. 19:1 in the *NWT* talks of 'a great crowd IN HEAVEN.'

Scripture shows that not only is there no link between the little flock and the 144,000, but also that the 144,000 cannot be who the Society says they are. The Society teaches that the 144,000 are in heaven and the great crowd on earth but the Scriptures teach that the 144,000 are on earth and the great crowd are in heaven.

The numerical problem

Another problem that the Watchtower has over the 144,000 is knowing when the numbering started and ended.

> But Jesus' resurrection to spirit life in the heavens opened up a new way of hope for his followers. After Jesus died and was resurrected men and women could be set aside to become the 'little flock' of 144,000 persons who make up the heavenly, spiritual nation of God. (*From Paradise Lost to Paradise Regained*, WBTS, 1958, p. 231)

> However, each year, on the anniversary of Christ's death the few remaining members of the 'little flock' yet on earth keep the Memorial of Christ's death. (*The Truth that Leads to Eternal Life*, WBTS, 1968, p. 80)

Question: How did the WBTS know the number of places left of the 144,000 when it began in the 1870's?

Question: Why has the number of the 144,000 left on earth gone up over the last six years? The number should decrease as these older members die but look at the figures recorded in the 1 January *Watchtowers* over the past five years.

1993 – 8683	1996 – 8645
1994 – 8693	1997 – 8757
1995 – 8617	1998 – 8795

Since 1931 the Right Shepherd has been gathering his 'other sheep'. So the hundreds of thousands of persons now associating with the New World society are 'other sheep'. (*From Paradise Lost to Paradise Regained*, WBTS, 1958, p. 195)

People with the Scriptural hope of everlasting life in an earthly paradise have been benefited. Since the momentous year of 1935 CE they have come out of all nations... (*Man's Salvation Out Of World Distress At Hand*, 1975, p. 302)

Question: How could there be a mistake over this number if God is in control? In a book published in 1958, we are told the number was complete in 1931 but in a book published in 1975, we are told 1935!

There is a further fundamental question about the number of the 144,000, 'Can they be less than the other sheep?' The Society teaches that the 144,000 alone are in the New Covenant but is this scripturally possible? Former Witness Phil Mawson felt that it was not possible when he studied the Scriptures.

Gal. 4:22-31 mentions how Abraham had two sons, one by Hagar the bondwoman and another by Sarah the free woman, Ishmael and Isaac respectively. Verse 24 in the *NWT*, reads that these two women, 'stand as symbolic drama, for these women mean TWO COVENANTS.' Verses 24 & 25 tell us that Hagar symbolises the Old Law Covenant from Sinai, and verses 26 & 27 that Sarah stands for the New Covenant and the Jerusalem above our [the Christian's] mother. Then in verse 27 Paul quotes from Is. 54:1 where Jehovah God is married to the nation of Israel via the Law Covenant. Compare also Jer. 3:14, 31:33.

Thus the barren or desolate woman which represents the New Covenant, has many more children (NKJV) or MORE NUMEROUS (*NWT*) than the woman who has the husband. The latter represents the old Law Covenant between Israel and Jehovah.

It is therefore very clear that if this old Law Covenant brought forth millions of children from the time of Moses to John the Baptist (Matt. 11:13); the New Covenant would bring forth many more than this, yes they would be more numerous. Thus, scripture demonstrates that the New Covenant is made with millions of persons, and not just 144,000 as is taught by the Watchtower.

Conclusion

All the biblical evidence shows that the 144,000 cannot be who the Society says they are but the question remains, who are they?

The Watchtower teaches that Israel has been rejected forever because they rejected Jesus. However, Scripture tells of a time when God will again show favour to the Jews and many will be saved (see Rom. 10-11; Zech. 12:10-14; Rev. 1:7). Though God's day of wrath is devastating (Zeph. 1:2-3,14,18), survival is possible (Zeph. 2:1-3). Some Jews will be saved 'through the fire' (Zech. 13:8-9), and this could well correspond with the protective sealing of the Jews in Rev. 7. Some believe that the group of 144,000 represents the remnant mentioned in Rom. 10 and 11.

The great crowd

What does the Society teach about the great crowd and especially where it is going to spend eternal life? Is it in a different place to the 144,000 or are they in the same place?

In the *WT*, 1 November 1974, pp. 666-67, we have the picture of Noah's ark. Noah represents Jesus, Noah's wife represents the 144,000, and Noah's sons and wives represent the 'great crowd' of 'other sheep'. In this picture they are all in the same place; they all pass through the same judgement; and they all have the same destination! How is this possible if they are going to end up in two distinct places? Alternatively, is the picture right in that they all will be in the same place?

The new covenant

The new covenant will terminate with the glorification of the remnant who are today in that covenant mediated by Christ. The 'great crowd' of 'other sheep' that is forming today is not in that new covenant. However by their associating with the 'little flock' of those yet in that covenant they come under the benefits that flow from that new covenant. (*WT*, 1 April 1979, p. 31)

There is one God, and one mediator between God and men (not, all men), a man Christ Jesus, who gave himself a corresponding ransom for all ... Evidently the new covenant is nearing the end of its operation for the purpose of producing 144,000 spiritual Israelites... When the last of these approved spiritual Israelites cease to be 'men' because of earthly death and a resurrection to share in the heavenly kingdom, then the mediatorship of Jesus Christ will cease also. (*WT*, 15 November 1979, pp. 26-27)

These quotes leave more questions than they answer. If the 'other sheep' are not in the new covenant which one are they in? They cannot be in the old because that has ended. So, where are they?

We must also ask how, when the new covenant ends, can my sins be forgiven? The answer is, if the mediatorship of Jesus will cease, as the above quote tells me, they cannot be. Even if it were true that they can get benefits by associating with the 'little flock,' the latter cannot mediate for the 'other sheep' nor forgive sins.

The Watchtower teaches that the Old Covenant has been replaced and that the New Covenant alone provides forgiveness of sin.

> The new covenant, which is made operative by Jesus' shed blood, replaces the old Law covenant. It is mediated by Jesus Christ between two parties-on the one hand, Jehovah God, and on the other, 144,000 spirit-begotten Christians. Besides providing for forgiveness of sins, the covenant allows for the formation of a heavenly nation of king-priests. (*WT*, 1 July 1990, p. 9)

These articles are very revealing and if we study them we discover, as indeed the Bible teaches, that all are in one ark and all are going to be in the same place. When we read the last chapters of the Bible we find that heaven and earth (the places of the 144,000 and the great crowd according to the Society) are rolled into one and all are indeed in the same place.

We also discover that as they are not in the Old Covenant they must be in the New or nothing at all. The fact that they are going to have any hope is because Jesus is still mediating, despite what the Watchtower try to say, for all men (1 Tim 2:5), and not just a small group. The New Covenant will never finish and we do not have to get man or even 144,000 spiritual ones to mediate for us because Jesus is still there.

Conclusion

This section shows conclusively that the Bible does not teach a two-tier reward for eternal life. There is no separation of a small group in heaven and a large group on earth with an impassable divide down the middle.

11

The Word of God

— ◎ —

The New World Translation
A look at the literature of the WBTS leaves us with the impression that it believes the whole of the Bible to be God's Word and that as a Society it only teaches scriptural doctrines.

The claim
> It is of vital importance to them [Jehovah's Witnesses] that their beliefs be based on the Bible and not on mere human speculations or religious creeds. (*Jehovah's Witnesses In The Twentieth Century*, 1979, p. 3)

> They [Jehovah's Witnesses] rely on both the Greek and the Hebrew Scriptures, and take them literally except where the expressions or settings obviously indicate that they are figurative or symbolical. (*ibid.*, p. 4)

> The *Kingdom Interlinear Translation* can serve as a safeguard against error in these days when many religious leaders are teaching twisted things, even twisting the written Word of God ... by going to *The Kingdom Interlinear Translation of the Greek Scriptures*, a student can go to THE ORIGINAL BIBLE TEXT ... (*WT*, 15 November 1969, p. 696)

> Never forget that THE BIBLE IS OUR STANDARD and that however God-given our helps may be they are 'HELPS' AND NOT SUBSTITUTES FOR THE BIBLE. (*WTR*, 15 December 1909, p. 4531)

To get understanding and other benefits, a person must approach the reading of God's Word with an open mind, THROWING ASIDE ALL PREJUDICE AND PRECONCEIVED OPINIONS; otherwise his understanding will be veiled. (*Insight*, Vol. 2, p. 755)

Bible students?

The above quotes show that Jehovah's Witnesses think of themselves as 'Bible Students.' This indeed was their name for many years and to the outsider they still give the impression of knowing their Bibles and having an apparently biblical answer for every question fired at them.

But are Jehovah's Witnesses really Bible students? We will look at some further quotes from the Society's publications.

No time for any Bible study in depth

The Society suggests that deep research is unnecessary.

> We may think of study as hard work, as involving heavy research. But in Jehovah's organization it is not necessary to spend a lot of time and energy in research, for there are brothers in the organization who are assigned to do that very thing, to help you who do not have so much time for this, these preparing the good material in *The Watchtower* and other publications of the Society. (*WT*, 1 June 1967, p. 338)

The majority of time is therefore spent in studying publications that explain the Bible the Watchtower way.

The only channel

> Jehovah's organization as directed by his 'faithful and discreet slave' class should influence our every decision. How may we avail ourselves of this good influence? By doing personal research in the Bible publications of the

Watch Tower Bible and Tract Society on whatever subject our decision concerns. (*WT*, 15 March 1969, p. 172)

Witnesses should do the majority of their studying from Watchtower publications.

Cannot understand without the organisation

He [God] does not impart his holy spirit and an understanding and appreciation of his Word apart from his visible organization. (*WT*, 1 July 1965, p. 391)

Jehovah God caused the Bible to be written in such a way that one needs to come in touch with His human channel before one can fully and accurately understand it. True, we need the help of God's holy spirit, but its help also comes to us primarily by association with the channel Jehovah God sees fit to use. (*WT*, 15 February 1981, p. 17)

Unless we are in touch with this channel of communication that God is using, we will not progress along the road to life, no matter how much Bible reading we do. (*WT*, 1 December 1981, p. 27)

The Bible is an organizational book and belongs to the Christian congregation as an organization, NOT TO INDIVIDUALS, regardless of how sincerely they may believe that they can interpret the Bible. For this reason the Bible cannot be properly understood without Jehovah's visible organization in mind. (*WT*, 1 October 1967, p. 587)

The Bereans

The Society even manage to twist the Scripture about the Bereans in Acts 17 to its own way of thinking. The Scripture says of them,

... [they] were more noble-minded than those in Thessalonica, for they received the word with the greatest eagerness of mind, carefully examining the Scriptures daily as to whether these things were so. Therefore many of them became believers ... (Acts 17:11-12, *NWT*)

The Watchtower says, however,

These Bereans listened with a readiness, yes, an eagerness, to believe. Thus not only were they open-minded, but they were wanting to have this 'good news' proved true. In fact, for a person to acquire faith he must have 'the will to believe' ... BUT NOWHERE DO WE READ THAT THOSE BROTHERS FIRST, IN A SKEPTICAL FRAME OF MIND, CHECKED THE SCRIPTURES TO MAKE CERTAIN THAT THOSE LETTERS HAD SCRIPTURAL BACKING, THAT THE WRITERS REALLY KNEW WHAT THEY WERE TALKING ABOUT ... No question about it. We all need help to understand the Bible, and we cannot find the Scriptural guidance we need outside the 'faithful and discreet slave' organization. (*WT*, 15 February 1981, pp. 18-19)

An accidental admission

Does the understanding given by the Watchtower publications on biblical matters match an understanding of the Bible if read without Watchtower guidance?

They say [those who leave the Watchtower Society] that it is sufficient to read the Bible exclusively, either alone or in small groups at home. But, strangely, through such 'Bible reading,' they have reverted right back to the apostate doctrines that commentaries by Christendom's clergy were teaching 100 years ago ... (*WT*, 15 August 1981, pp. 28-29)

If you read the Bible without Watchtower guidance, you would come to believe what Christendom's clergy have been teaching all along. A normal reading of the Bible would take a person away from the teachings of the Society.

Check it out

We need to do what the Society asks us (*WT*, 15 November 1969) and check its English translation with the Greek in the KIT. Below are a few examples of the type of changes we find. The KIT literal Greek is shown first and underneath the *NWT* with changes in bold type.

1 Cor. 10:4	was the Christ
	meant the Christ
Rev. 3:14	beginning of the creation of the God
	the beginning of the creation **by** God
1 John 4:2	the spirit of God
	inspired expression from God
John 17:3	that they may be knowing you the only true God
	their **taking in knowledge** of you the only true God
John 1:4	in him life was
	by means of him was life
John 13:31	and the God was glorified in him
	and God is glorified **in connection with** him
Heb. 9:27	it is reserved for men once to die after but this (thing) judgement
	it is reserved for men to die once **for all** time but after this a judgement
Acts 10:36	Jesus Christ: this One is of all (them) Lord
	Jesus Christ: this One is Lord of all [others]
Heb. 12:23	and to spirits of righteous (ones)
	and **the spiritual lives** of righteous ones

Above all, a careful study of the *NWT* and especially the *KIT* shows that the Society is guilty of twisting God's Word. We give a couple of examples here but further details can be found in Reachout's leaflet *Examining the Watchtower Bible*.

John 1:1. The *KIT* appendix (pp. 1158-60) explains that *theos* is rendered here as 'a god' because it is 'anarthrous,' that is without the Greek definite article *ho*. This 'principle of translation' should be applied consistently, but is it?

In Mark 12:26-27 the anarthrous *theos* is rendered twice as 'God' and once as 'a God.' Only sixteen times out of 282 occurrences of the anarthrous *theos* does the *NWT* render it as 'god,' 'a god,' 'gods,' or 'godly.' This means the Society made up its own rule and then broke it ninety-four times out of a hundred.

Col. 1:27-28. 'Union with' are two words, which are added many times in the New Testament but are not in the Greek. The Society will not accept that Jesus can be 'in' us or we can be 'in Christ.' Therefore, it adds to God's Word to prevent Jehovah's Witnesses having a personal relationship with Jesus Christ. However, John 17:26 shows clearly the society's inconsistency in translating *en autois*.

> And I have made your name known to them and will make it known, in order that the love with which you loved me may be in them (*en autois*) and I in UNION WITH them (*en autois*). (*NWT*)

In the same verse, the Society translates 'in' and 'in union with' but the Greek is the same. We can have 'God's love' in us but not Jesus Christ. This inconsistency occurs over ninety times. The Society is guilty of inconsistency in translation because of the need to support a specific viewpoint.

Who is the Lord?
In a number of passages, the Watchtower causes confusion by its translation of the Greek word for Lord, *kyrios* in all its various forms. We have listed a few below.

...Stephen ... made appeal and said: 'Lord Jesus [*Kyrie Iesou*] receive my spirit.' Then ... he cried out with a strong voice: 'Jehovah [*Kyrie*] do not charge this sin against them.' (Acts 7:59-60, *NWT*)

The second *kyrie* translated as Jehovah seeks to divide Jesus from Jehovah. Whilst this suits Watchtower doctrine there is no such distinction in the Greek.

Whatever you are doing, work at it whole-souled as to Jehovah [*kyrio*], and not to men, for you know that it is from Jehovah [*kyrion*] you will receive the due reward of the inheritance. Slave for the Master, Christ [*kyrio Christo*]. (Col. 3:23,24, *NWT*)

Twice *kyrio* is translated 'Jehovah' but the third as 'master'. It is strange that if we are serving Jehovah we are also to serve (slave for) the Lord Christ, especially when Jesus said it is impossible to serve two masters (Matt. 6:24). For Christians there is no problem! Jesus is Lord, just as Yahweh is Lord, they are both God. Therefore, service to the Lord is service to God the Father and Jesus because they are one.

... for both if we live, we live to Jehovah [*kyrio*], and if we die, we die to Jehovah [*kyrio*]. Therefore, both if we live and if we die, we belong to Jehovah [*kyrion*]. For to this end Christ died and came to life again, that he might be Lord [*kyrieuse*] over both the dead and the living. (Rom. 14:8-9, *NWT*)

In verse 8, the *NWT* translates *kyrio* Jehovah, but if Jehovah is our Lord whether we live or die, how can Jesus be Lord of the dead and living unless He is God?

Jesus and the end times

Again the choice of translation by the Watchtower is under-lined by 1 Thess. 4:15-17. The Watchtower uses these verses as part of its proof that Jesus is Michael the Archangel but they are very interesting for other reasons.

> For this is what we tell you by Jehovah's word ... because the Lord himself will descend from heaven ... and those who are dead in union with Christ will rise first. Afterward we the living who are surviving will, together with them, be caught away in clouds to meet the Lord in the air; and thus we shall always be with [the] Lord. (*NWT*)

These events will take place together, therefore if Jesus returned in 1914, as the Watchtower believes, the dead in union with Christ rose and the living were caught away at that time. This is not what the WBTS believes, however.

It also uses 'Lord' again in these verses. As we explain (p. 211) when discussing the 'Name of Jehovah' the Society uses a number of other Bible translations, each given a 'J' number, to help it decide which word to use. These verses are a classic example of the 'pick and mix' translation of the Watchtower.

In verse 15 the *NWT* informs us that J7,8,17,18 all have 'Jehovah' and therefore it can too. We are informed about verses 16 & 17 that J7, 8, 13, 14 all have 'Jehovah' but it prefers 'Lord'. Why are two of these references right for verse 15 but wrong for verses 16 & 17? Jesus would be called by the name of Jehovah!

Scholars and the *New World Translation*

The WBTS wants us to believe that scholars approve and support its translation of the Bible. In a letter from the Society (London, 26 September 1985, ref.: EC:SE) it gives a number of quotes to prove this. We list them below. As usual, the parts the

Society left out are supplied in bold letters. The quotes are introduced in the letter as follows:

> Finally, we felt it might be of some assistance to list a few comments by various scholars concerning the *New World Translation* particularly highlighting the competence of its translators:

> The translation has been endorsed by no less an authority than C. H. Dodd ... Referring to 'the Word was a god' he states: 'If translation were a matter of substituting words, a possible translation of [John 1:1] would be, "The Word was a god". As a word-for-word translation it cannot be faulted ... **The reason why it is unacceptable is that it runs counter to the current of Johanine thought, and indeed of Christian thought as a whole.'** (*The Bible Translator*, January 1997, Vol. 28, pp. 101-102)

> Samuel Haas said of the *New World Translation*, **'While this work** indicates a great deal of effort and thought as well as considerable scholarship, **it is to be regretted that religious bias was allowed to colour many passages'.** (*Journal of Biblical Literature*, December 1955, p. 283)

> Robert M. McCoy said: **'In not a few instances the *New World Translation* contains passages which must be considered as "theological translations" ... John 8:58... On grammatical grounds alone ... cannot be justified. It cannot be called a historical present, since the words are not narrative ...** The translation of the New Testament is evidence of the presence in the movement of scholars qualified to deal intelligently with the many problems of Biblical translation'. (*Andover Newton Quarterly*, 3,1963, pp. 29-31)

Professor Bruce M. Metzger: 'On the whole one gains a tolerably good impression of the scholarly equipment of the translators (their names are not divulged) ... **Some of the translations which are simply indefensible ... The introduction of the word "Jehovah" into the New Testament ... John 1:1 ... is not justified despite a lengthy note... the translators have not hesitated to insert four times the word "other" (totally without warrant from the Greek) ... in Col[ossians] 1:16f'.** (The Bible Translator, Vol. 15, 1964, pp. 151-52)

S. Maclean Gilmour, Norris Professor of New Testament: 'The New Testament translation was made by a committee whose membership has never been revealed – a committee that possessed an unusual competence in Greek **... It is clear that doctrinal considerations influenced many turns of phrase ...**' (*Andover Newton Quarterly*, 1966, pp. 25-26)

Even the scholars that the WBTS quote do not support the *New World Translation*. However, there are other scholars we should also note because of their contact with the Society.

Julius R. Mantey, quoted by the Society as supporting the *NWT*, said:

There is no statement in our Grammar that was ever meant to imply that 'a god' was a permissible translation ... because you have been quoting me out of context, I herewith request you not quote the manua l... again. (Letter to the Watchtower Society dated 11 July 1974)

Dr A. T. Robertson is also quoted as supporting the Society's view, but wrote 'This [Romans 9:5] is atrociously mistranslated in the *NWT*... I disagree radically with this statement in the *KIT*.' (*Word Pictures*, Vol. 4, p. 381)

Another source quoted in both the *Watchtower* and *All*

Scripture is Inspired of God and Beneficial is Professor Benjamin Kedar of Israel.

> In fact, the *New World Translation* is a scholarly work. In 1989, Professor Benjamin Kedar of Israel said: 'In my linguistic research in connection with the Hebrew Bible and translations, I often refer to the English edition of what is known as the *New World Translation*. In so doing, I find my feeling repeatedly confirmed that this work reflects an honest endeavour to achieve an understanding of the text that is as accurate as possible. Giving evidence of a broad command of the original language, it renders the original words into a second language understandably without deviating unnecessarily from the specific structure of the Hebrew ... Every statement of language allows for a certain latitude in interpreting or translating. So the linguistic solution in any given case may be open to debate. But I have never discovered in the *New World Translation* any biased intent to read something into the text that it does not contain.

The author has two personal letters from Prof. Dr. Kedar who is a research fellow of the Hebrew University Bible Project. An extract from his first letter reads as follows:

> It is evident that I do not share the tenets of so-called Jehova's [sic] Witnesses, i.e. the Watchtower people, but I absolutely have no wish to get involved in sectarian jealousies and quibbles. A quite different question is that of their Bible translation, the *New World Translation*. I have checked hundreds of verses and have never found what one may consider a tendentious misinterpretation of the Hebrew text of the Old Testament. (Haifa, 1 March 1992)

As most of the major problem verses are in the New Testament anyway I wrote back and asked about the Greek and especially putting 'Jehovah' back into the New Testament. The reply is as follows:

> As you have correctly stated all my pronouncements on the Watchtower version refer exclusively to the Hebrew portion of the Bible, i.e. the Old Testament, of which I have checked hundreds of verses. I am not qualified to pass judgement on the correspondent English version of the Greek New Testament. As to the name 'Jehovah' you certainly are aware of the fact that such pronunciation of the tetragrammaton YHWH is absolutely erroneous... as to [sic] the Greek rendition of this name ... I am sure somebody has informed the Witnesses of their blunder but they obviously find it hard – as all of us do – to abandon a tradition just because of scholarly objections. (Haifa, 9 May, 1992)

The Watchtower has not, to date, produced one biblical scholar of good reputation to support its translation, whereas many more than are quoted here have condemned it for one reason or another.

12

1914 then and now

— ଲ —

Chronology

From the beginning the WBTS has been fascinated with dates. Russell's fascination with the dating of the Adventist movement was the inspiration to start the Watchtower. Many are also aware of the different dates that have been given for the 'end of the world.' This may not seem such an important issue to those outside the Society but if you are a Jehovah's Witness then you will be aware of phrases such as 'God's absolute date.'

Although the dates may have changed and indeed what was supposed to have happened on various dates, one number has always remained constant – 1914. This becomes the pivotal point of the Watchtower belief covering both the 'return' of Jesus Christ and the starting point to date the 'end of the world.' But there are no dates within the Bible, so how does the Society arrive at this number? The answer is chronology, and an understanding of it is helpful when talking with a Witness about these things.

In summary the Watchtower chronology goes like this:

1. An absolute date, which must be an event both in the Bible and in secular history, is decided upon. The Watchtower chose the fall of Babylon in 539 BC.
2. Now turning to the Bible alone it says that two years later, 537 BC, Cyrus decreed that the Jews could return to Jerusalem.

3. This means that 537 is the end of Jerusalem's seventy years of desolation, which therefore began at its fall in 607 BC.
4. Daniel's dream in chapter 4 and the 'Bible rule' that a day equals a year, show that the Gentile Times, which began at Jerusalem's fall in 607 BC, would be 2520 years long, ending in 1914.

For those with a head for numbers you can investigate the subject in more depth in the Additional Study section on p. 221.

What did Russell say about 1914?

There are many quotations in Watchtower literature that show how modern-day Witnesses think about the prophecies regarding 1914.

> Consider, too, the fact that Jehovah's organization alone, in all the earth, is directed by God's holy spirit ... Direction by God's spirit enables Jehovah's servants TO HAVE DIVINE LIGHT ... For instance, long ago they understood that 1914 CE would mark the end of the Gentile Times or 'appointed times of the nations'... *Zion's Watch Tower* of March 1880 had declared: 'The Times of the Gentiles extend to 1914, and the heavenly kingdom will not have full sway till then'. (*WT*, 1 July 1973, p. 402)

> From the outset, the *Watch Tower* showed that at Christ's second coming his parousia would be an invisible presence as a mighty spirit person ... this journal's early issues (March and June 1880) pointed to 1914 CE as a climactic year. It was to mark the close of the 2,520-year-long Gentile Times, during which non-Jewish nations would rule the earth without interference by any kingdom of God. (*WT*, 1 July 1979, p. 5)

> By the date of October 1 of 1914 World War I had been raging for more than two months ... Who were the ones

that, many years beforehand, pointed out... that 'the Times of the Gentiles' would end in the latter half of 1914? It was the International Bible Students... Today they are known world-wide as Jehovah's Witnesses ... have those opposers who far outnumber Jehovah's Witnesses won the hot dispute concerning the setting up of God's Kingdom by Christ in the heavens in 1914 CE... No! (*WT*, 1 January 1983, pp. 10-11)

To summarise, the Watchtower makes the following claims concerning its past 'prophetic' statements:

1. With its 'Divine Light' it pointed to 1914 as a special year, more so than any other year it named.
2. The 'Gentile Times' would end by 1 October 1914.
3. Christ's kingdom would be a heavenly one.
4. Christ's kingdom would start in 1914.
5. Christ's coming would be an invisible one.

1914 has been a corner stone to Watchtower 'theology' for over 100 years but what did C. T. Russell actually say in the early publications of the WBTS?

But, 'If I go away, I will come again,' cannot refer to a spiritual coming again, because, spiritually, He never went away, as He said, 'Lo, I am with you alway, even to the end of the world,' [age]. Therefore, Jesus taught His second PERSONAL coming. (*ZWTR*, July 1879, p. 4, emphasis in the original)

'The Times of the Gentiles' extend to 1914, and the heavenly Kingdom will not have full sway till then, but as a 'Stone' the kingdom of God is set up 'in the days of these (ten Gentile) kings,' and by consuming them it becomes a universal kingdom – a 'great mountain and FILLS THE WHOLE EARTH'. (*ZWTR*, March 1880, p. 82)

The presence (of the Bridegroom)... began in the fall of 1874. (*ZWTR*, April 1880, p. 87)

True, it is expecting great things to claim, as we do, that within the coming twenty-six years all present governments will be overthrown and dissolved ... In view of this strong Bible evidence ... we consider it an established truth that the FINAL END of the kingdoms of THIS WORLD, and the FULL ESTABLISHMENT of the Kingdom of God, will be accomplished by the end of 1914 AD. (*The Divine Plan of the Ages*, WBTS, 1889, pp. 98-99)

The date of the CLOSE of that 'battle' is definitely marked in Scripture as October, 1914. It is already in progress, its beginning dating from October, 1874. (*ZWTR*, 15 January 1892, p. 1355)

The CULMINATION OF THE TROUBLE in October, 1914 is clearly marked in the Scriptures; and we are bound therefore to expect a beginning of that severe trouble NOT LATER THAN 1910. (*ZWTR*, 15 September 1901, p. 2876)

The final spasm, which WE LOOK FOR IN 1915, will give birth to the new dispensation of peace and blessing, the Millennial reign of Messiah. (*ZWTR*, 1 January 1908, p. 4111)

Finally, let us remember that we did not consecrate either to October 1914, nor to October 1915, nor to any other date, but 'unto death'. (*WTR*, 1 December 1912, p. 5142)

Indeed, as respects the date 1914, which we have emphasized, and respecting which we have repeatedly expressed our faith, our conviction – even respecting this date we have never knowingly spoken IN INFALLIBLE TERMS. We have always admitted that it is a matter of faith and conviction, RATHER THAN ABSOLUTE KNOWLEDGE. (*WTR*, 1 June 1913, p. 5249)

Only one thing did the Editor fear in respect to the influences mentioned and the able addresses of the speakers. He fears that the dear friends in several instances were over-stimulated by TOO POSITIVE ASSURANCE that the present year will witness the 'change' of the church, establishment of the kingdom etc .... At no time has the Editor ever spoken or written as POSITIVELY as some of these dear brethren are speaking now. In the books, Studies in the Scriptures, as well as in the Watch Tower, we have set forth the chronology, NOT AS INFALLIBLE, but nevertheless declared our confidence in it ... In recent numbers of The Watch Tower we have plainly stated that fulfilments of the prophecies, although marked and manifest, ARE NOT AS FAR DEVELOPED FOR THE TIME AS WE HAD EXPECTED. (*WTR*, 15 July 1914, p. 5502)

September 20 of this year, 1914 PROBABLY marked the end of the Gentile times. (*WTR*, 1 November 1914, p. 5566)

We see no reason for doubting, therefore, that the Times of Gentiles ended in October, 1914; and that A FEW MORE YEARS will witness their utter collapse and the full establishment of God's kingdom in the hands of Messiah ... OUR MISTAKE WAS ... that some historians put the end of the Jewish Time of Trouble as April AD 73, which would correspond to April 1918. (*WTR*, 1 September 1916, pp. 5950-51)

These statements are but the tip of the iceberg as far as the early chronology of the Society is concerned but from these we can draw the following comparisons with the modern-day claims.

1. Russell did not point exclusively to 1914 and the nearer 1914 came the more Russell doubted his original 'prophecies.'
2. Russell first said that the 'Gentile Times' ended on 20 September 1914, and later saw 'no reason for doubting' October 1914.
3. Russell always said that the kingdom would be an earthly one. What the Witnesses teach today about Christ's invisible reign has nothing to do with Russell's teaching of the end of the world's governmental systems.
4. Neither by December 1914, nor by his death in 1916, had Russell received the 'light' that God had promised to his true children and not once did he claim that the kingdom was set up in 1914.
5. The very first issue of *ZWTR* clearly taught Christ's personal coming. This view has been slowly modified over the years.

Above all, Russell himself warned that these were only suggestions and not a prophetic warning concerning 1914. Although he was still alive some two years into World War I, Russell never claimed any significance to it. Yet today the Society shows that event, above all else, as 'proving' Russell's 'prophecies.'

Modern-day changes

We have seen that the Watchtower has changed Russell's teaching on 1914 to put it in a favourable light. However, in *The Watchtowers* of 15 October and 15 November 1995 it made another major change concerning 1914. In these issues 'the generation,' that had been 'tinkered' with over the years received a major deathblow.

This is the generation in Matt. 24 that would see the end of this world, as we know it or in Watchtower language, 'this system of things'. The teaching had been that the generation that saw the events of 1914 would not pass away until God set up His Kingdom on earth. There had been minor changes over the years as the following quotes show.

Jesus was obviously speaking about those who were old enough to witness with understanding what took place when the 'last days' began. (*Aw.*, 8 October 1968, p. 13)

Thus, when it comes to the application in our time, the 'generation' logically would not apply to babies born during World war I. It applies to Christ's followers and others who were able to observe that war ... (*WT*, 1 October 1978, p. 31)

If Jesus used 'generation' in that sense and we apply it to 1914, then the babies of that generation are now 70 years old or older. And others alive in 1914 are in their 80's or 90's, a few even having reached a hundred. (*WT*, 15 May 1984, p. 5)

Despite these changes, the end was still in sight for the generation of 1914 and the Watchtower had to make a radical change if it was not to be found out to be a false prophet again. This took place in November 1995 and now there is no apparent end in sight for the generation.

The Watchtower Society is now saying that although Jehovah gave the sign of the wars, earthquakes etc. in Matt. 24:3, He did not give the exact date that He would execute judgement. This is borne out by the first fulfilment of this prophecy with the Jews and the destruction of Jerusalem.

From Daniel's prophecy, the Jews could have calculated the timing of Jesus' appearing as the Messiah. (Dan. 9:25) Yet they were given no date for the 'great tribulation' that finally destroyed the apostate Jewish system of things. It was only after the destruction of Jerusalem and its temple that they realized that the date was 70 CE. (*WT*, 1 November 1995, p. 11)

The outcome is that the Society can no longer say that it will be in 1975 or 1999 or any date because no one knows that hour and we will not know until after the event. This is a remarkable turn around when you consider some of the articles it has published in the past. For instance, *The Watchtower* of 1 April 1984 led with the article *1914 A Marked Year – Why?*, much of the reasoning behind it being a marked year centred on the 'signs of the times.' Now they mean nothing. Previous editions of *Awake! to the Watchtower* have included a chapter on the way the Society falsified the records over the 'Signs' of wars, earthquakes etc. This is now not a major factor as it is not pinpointing the signs as taking effect in 1914 but is 'playing down' the claims.

> Since 1914 CE, there has been an increase in the number of earthquakes, resulting in much distress. (*Insight*, Vol. 1 p. 670)

Surely we can still say that it is soon because the generation will soon die out and it must happen before then? No, even that has changed.

> ... the masses of unrepentant Jews of that time obviously made up 'this adulterous and sinful generation' ... What, then, is the 'generation' so frequently referred to by Jesus in the presence of his disciples? What did they understand by his words ... Surely, Jesus was not departing from his established use of the term ... which he constantly applied to the contemporary masses with their 'blind guides' who together made up the Jewish nation.' (*WT*, 1 November 1995, pp. 13, 14)

The generation is no longer the one that saw 1914 but it is 'today's generation'. In addition, as long as this world exists it will be 'today's generation.' With this change comes another difference. Witnesses have always been taught that chronology and dating are a vital part of the proof that Jesus returned invisibly in 1914. This key to the 'truth' is apparently now not so important; in fact, it is not necessary for salvation at all.

> Those Jews who had paid attention to Jesus' prophetic words realized that their salvation depended, not on trying to calculate the length of a 'generation' or of some dated 'times and seasons,' but on keeping separate from the evil contemporary generation and zealously doing God's will. (*WT*, 1 November 1995, p. 15)

The society indeed clearly states,

> We do not need to know the exact timing of events. Rather, our focus must be on being watchful, cultivating strong faith, and keeping busy in Jehovah's service – not on calculating a date. (*WT*, 1 November 1995, p. 17)

On some things it never changes, we must still be busy in Jehovah's service but I wonder how can you have strong faith in an organisation that makes such far reaching changes that alter the whole foundation it is built on.

But hasn't the Watchtower Society been guilty of date calculation? Yes, it admits that at least Jehovah's people have been guilty of this, if not the Governing Body!

> Eager to see the end of this evil system, Jehovah's people have at times speculated about the time when the 'great tribulation' would break out, even tying this to calculations of what is the lifetime of a generation since 1914. However, we 'bring a heart of wisdom in,' not by speculating about how many years or days make up a generation, but by thinking about how we 'count our days' in bringing joyful praise to Jehovah. (*WT*, 1 November 1995, p. 17)

Having so completely devastated the Jehovah's Witnesses, the leaders must try to give them some remaining hope. They must also try to give them some motivation to be out on the doors. To do this we read,

> Does our more precise viewpoint on 'this generation' mean that Armageddon is further away that we had thought? Not at all! Though we at no time have known the 'day and hour,' Jehovah God has always known it, and he does not change. (*WT*, 1 November 1995, p. 20)

(See also *WT*, 1 April 1997, pp. 14-18 and probably many other such articles in the future.)

The Society will of course try to show that this change is 'new light' or that it is tacking in a sailboat. In *WT*, 1 December 1981, p. 27, we read,

> At times explanations given by Jehovah's visible organization have shown adjustments, seemingly to, previous points of view. But this has not actually been the case. This might be compared to what is known in navigational circles as 'tacking.' By manoeuvring the sails the sailors can cause a ship to go from right to left, back and forth, but all the time making progress toward their destination in spite of contrary winds.

We can show that neither of these explanations fit this scenario because there has not been a change to an idea of man but the change has been to a promise of Jehovah. Note the two quotations below; the first is taken from the *Awake!* 22 October 1995 and the second from *Awake!* 8 November 1995.

> *Awake!* Is for the enlightenment of the entire family. It shows how to cope with today's problems. It reports the news, tells about people in many lands, examines religion and science. But it does more. It probes beneath the

surface and points to the real meaning behind current events, yet it always stays politically neutral and does not exalt one race above another. Most important, this magazine builds confidence in the Creator's promise of a peaceful and secure new world BEFORE THE GENERATION THAT SAW THE EVENTS OF 1914 PASSES AWAY.

Awake! Is for the enlightenment of the entire family. It shows how to cope with today's problems. It reports the news, tells about people in many lands, examines religion and science. But it does more. It probes beneath the surface and points to the real meaning behind current events, yet it always stays politically neutral and does not exalt one race above another. Most important, this magazine builds confidence in the Creator's promise of a peaceful and secure new world THAT IS ABOUT TO REPLACE THE PRESENT WICKED, LAWLESS SYSTEM OF THINGS.

For any thinking Witness, this will give problems. Undoubtedly it did because the Society had to explain things afresh in a 'Questions from Readers' *WT*, 1 June 1997, p. 28. Referring back to the 1 November article, it answered 'That discussion in *The Watchtower*, offered no change at all in our fundamental teaching about 1914 ... '

At this point it even went back briefly to the 'signs' to prove that Jesus was King since 1914. The answer then went on to conclude,

> So the recent information ... did not change our understanding of what occurred in 1914. But it did give us a clearer grasp of Jesus' use of the term 'generation,' helping us to see that his usage was no basis for calculating – counting from 1914 – how close to the end we are.

This may satisfy the 'faithful' but there are major changes. How can a promise of Jehovah fail? Having answered that you would have to ask, was it a promise of Jehovah in the first place. Coming to the conclusion that it was not would lead to the conclusion that although the Society claims to be God's mouthpiece it is actually putting words into His mouth that He never said.

This change is also remarkable when you consider that in the *Awake!* 8 November 1994, referring to the reason for printing *Awake!*, the Society said,

> The fulfilment of Bible prophecy indicates that we have been living in the time of the end since 1914 ... This time of the end is, however, to be a relatively short period – stretching over one generation (Luke 21:31,32). The fact that we are now 80 years beyond 1914 indicates that we can soon expect the deliverance that God's Kingdom will bring. (Aw., 8 November 1994, p. 10)

Explain the changes

A message given by a Circuit Overseer in Lincoln in 1998 gives an interesting reason as to why the Society 'got it wrong' in times past and needed to make changes. Part of the transcript of this taped message reads:

> Why did Jehovah allow us for 120 years to misunderstand Matthew 24 v 34 about the Generation, why did he allow us, for he knew we got it wrong for 120 years, why? I tell you why, because we never, ever, ever would have gotten his preaching work done. Nobody would have been missionaries, nobody would have gone abroad, nobody would have pioneered, they would have all raised children, gone to university. There is a hundred years to go yet well no need to rush around ... you would not have been in the truth today and I wouldn't, because nobody would have bothered all that much, it was 120 years ago, isn't that right, marvellous you fooled me Jehovah, they got it wrong but it will do them good.

Can anyone really believe in a God that needs to 'fool' His people in order to get His work done? That is a deceptive god not the Jehovah of the Scripture. The tape goes on,

> Now here is the next question, why suddenly after 120 years has Jehovah revealed to us that we got it wrong, and given us the right understanding of the verse? Because the time is near and we need to show what is in our hearts. You've got it, now he wants to know what our real reason is now he has got us this far, it's his right. I've got you this far to the door, I now want to know what your motive is, are you going to stick with it, are you going to prove to be a sheep or a goat, amazing. What other organization after 120 years of getting it wrong, when they suddenly realize they got it wrong ... will let them know ... Isn't that right, the faithful and discreet organization.

In summary the Society is saying 'we got it wrong and we need to change it but who shall we blame?' In the end they did not take the blame themselves but said Jehovah fooled them. In all the excuses I have heard from the Society I believe this one is the worst and most insidious.

13

Social issues – blood

— ෴ —

The central issue here is the question of blood transfusions and whether God forbids them. As an individual, I have a right to refuse to take blood and that is not the issue we are investigating. We must answer the question as to whether the Society is right when it says that the Word of God forbids us from taking blood. First, we detail the development of this teaching in the Watchtower.

History

1909 C. T. Russell commented on Acts 15 that abstinence from these things would not make them Christians. The prohibition of the use of blood was necessary for the peace of the church. (*WTR*, 15 April, p. 4374)

1945 Blood transfusions were pronounced pagan and dishonouring to God. (*WT*, 1 July, pp. 198-201)

1958 The injection of antibodies into the blood or the use of blood fractions to create such antibodies is not the same as taking blood. It is a matter of individual judgement whether to accept such types of medication or not. (*WT*, 15 September, p. 575)

1959 The removal of one's blood, storing it and later putting it back into the same person is a violation of Scriptural principles. (*WT*, 15 October, p. 640)

1961 Having a blood transfusion is now a disfellowshipping offence. (*WT*, 15 January, pp. 63-64)

Donating organs (eyes) is a matter of conscience. (*WT*, 1 August, p. 480)

1963   Any fraction of blood considered as a nutrient is not to be used in medical treatment. Anything that is derived from blood and used to sustain life comes under this principle. (*WT*, 15 February, p. 124)

1967   Organ transplants are now considered cannibalism. (*WT*, 15 November, pp. 702-4)

1974   Serums are now a matter of conscience but believed to be wrong. (*WT'*, 1 June, p. 352)

1977   Blood transfusions are now considered as organ transplants. Many might decline blood simply because at best it is only partially compatible with their own blood. (*Jehovah's Witnesses and the Question of Blood*, 1977, p. 41)

1978   Taking a serum injection to fight against disease is not a clear-cut area. (*WT*, 15 June, pp. 30-31)

1980   Organ transplants are now made a matter of conscience. (*WT*, 15 March, p. 31)

1984   Bone-marrow transplant is now a matter of conscience but the way the Society argues the matter would lead a correctly trained conscience to say, no. (*WT*, 15 May, p. 31)

Blood transfusions

The Society claims that its Scriptural reasoning is based on, amongst others, the following three scriptures.

Gen. 9:4: 'Don't eat blood,' a law given to Noah and as we all come from Noah, a law for all mankind.

Lev. 17:10: an established Israelite law which if broken warranted death.

Acts 15:28-29: the law was also a Christian command.

It says that 'Christians are commanded to "abstain from blood" ... the eating of blood is equated with idolatry and fornication, things that we should not want to engage in.' (*Reasoning*, pp. 70-71) Blood transfusion is said to be the same as eating but by a quicker method. (*Jehovah's Witnesses and the Question of Blood*, 1977, pp. 17-18)

An alternative view

Acts 15:28-29 is the essential verse for Jehovah's Witnesses because it brings the matter of blood into the New Testament. Here we read that the Jewish elders in Jerusalem requested that the Gentiles do just four things and one of them was to 'abstain from blood.' However, just what did this mean? Obviously, it could not mean 'do not take blood transfusions' because they had not been developed.

This was written in the light of the Old Testament law on eating blood and the sacrifices. This is what it meant then, is it any different now? When did this verse change to include blood transfusions? It never has, this is something that the Society has added to try to boost its case.

If there is no justification in the New Testament Scripture the Old Testament ones need to be read in the context they were given.

Gen. 9:3-4. Though the Israelites could now eat meat, it had to be dead, without life left in it. The Watchtower makes this connection, even if accidentally.

> Jehovah God the Creator is responsible for the existence of all flesh, and for its life ... Originally, vegetation and fruit, and not flesh, were given man as his diet. But after the Flood God added animal flesh, commanding, however, that flesh with its soul – its blood – you must not eat... Cannibalism, the eating of human flesh, naturally was repugnant to the human mind, was abhorred by God and his ancient covenant people Israel. (*Insight*, Vol. l, p. 840)

Remember that we are dealing here with animals and animal blood. This was not to do with human blood but with the way that animals should be killed before they were eaten. Incidents such as occurred in Saul's day (1 Sam. 14:33) show that they should not eat the meat with the blood. There is no way that you can take God's law about not eating animal meat with its blood and make it say that God forbids blood transfusions.

Lev. 17:10. The Society says that it is no longer under Mosaic law, yet it continues to use this law. The law respecting blood also states 'It is a perpetual statute throughout your generation in all your dwellings: you shall not eat ANY FAT or any blood.' (Lev. 3:17, NASB) The Watchtower does not teach 'no fat' but why not, it is part of the same law?

Lev. 17:11 reads, 'FOR THE LIFE OF THE FLESH IS IN THE BLOOD, and I have given it to you on the altar to make atonement for your souls; for it is the blood by reason of the life that makes atonement.' (NASB)

The animals sacrificed on the altar, and especially the Passover Lamb, symbolised the coming of Jesus, 'the Lamb of God who takes away the sin of the world' (John 1:29). Heb. 9:20 says if there is no shed blood, there is no forgiveness. After Jesus shed His blood there were to be no more animal sacrifices on the altar, to make atonement, else we would be saying that Christ's death was not sufficient. Therefore, sacrifices passed away along with the pouring out of blood. (Lev. 17:13)

> By this will we have been sanctified through the offering of the body of Jesus Christ once for all. And every priest stands daily ministering and offering time after time the same sacrifices, which can never take away sins; but He [Jesus Christ], having offered one sacrifice for sins for all time, sat down at the right hand of God... (Heb 10:10-12, NASB)

What of blood transfusions?
The conclusions we draw from looking at these Scriptures in the light of all the Bible are:

1. The pouring out of blood is now unnecessary because that which it symbolised, the perfect sacrifice of Christ, has been made.
2. Jesus gave a ruling concerning legalistic dietary rules: 'Listen to Me, all of you, and understand: there is nothing outside the man which going into him can defile him; but the things which proceed out of the man are what defile the man ... (Thus He declared all foods clean.).' (Mark 7:14-19)
3. As the Society stresses that transfusing blood is the same as eating it, we should pay attention to Paul's words: 'But food will not commend us to God; we are neither the worse if we do not eat, nor the better if we do eat.' (1 Cor 8:8)

Hospital Liaison Committees

These committees (HLCs) have developed over recent years and are now an active part of the work of Witnesses in the community. The most 'charismatic' message I have ever heard from a member of the Society was from one of the founders of these committees sharing what could be done.

The HLC will write to every Hospital Management Committee to arrange to visit them, explaining the Witness stand on Blood and seeking to get the co-operation of doctors to perform operations without blood. When a Jehovah's Witness is taken into hospital and there may be the threat of a blood transfusion one of the local Liaison Committee will ring or visit and explain the different procedures the surgeons can use without blood.

Beyond this, the society has set up a register of doctors who will perform operations without blood and are willing to receive advice on the latest non-blood products. This has led to some compromises with 'Christendom' as can be seen from a report in *Hospital Doctor* dated 10 October 1991: 'In Chicago Witnesses have formed a bond with a CATHOLIC hospital which specialises in non-blood surgery.'

The Society is also compiling a register of solicitors. A letter sent out from the British headquarters lists the concerns that it would like the solicitors to be ready to undertake:

> The first concerns proposed blood transfusions for children. In elective surgery we are usually able to arrange referral to a surgeon who is prepared to operate on a child without homologous blood. However, there are cases, usually emergencies, when hospital authorities may combine with social services to try to override parental requests for alternative non-blood medical management. Our stand on the blood issue is non-negotiable and in these cases we are seeking committed representation.

Fortunately, in most cases involving minors the courts will take control and order the blood (see Note 1). Tragically, in adult cases they will not, and it is no exaggeration to say that hundreds die each year because of this. It is bad enough for the medical staff and family to have to cope with death at the best of times, but when they feel something could have been done it is tragic. Children do suffer, of course, because of the loss of parents, as the *Daily Telegraph* extract from early 1993 shows:

> Mrs Yvonne Leighton, 28, and her husband, Gordon, had signed forms refusing hospital staff permission to give her blood. Doctors had to stand by helplessly as she haemorrhaged during a simple operation for new mothers, 10 days after her son was born.

We of course are not advocating hating Witnesses because they do it. We understand that they believe they are laying down their lives for Jehovah's sake. Tragically, though, this is not true, because God has not forbidden it in the first place. I wonder if the elders of the local congregation realised the hurt and suffering they brought on the family and hospital staff? May this sort of instance challenge us more and more to love the Witnesses as they call at our doors.

We should also mention here an interesting court ruling at the Royal Courts of Justice, Monday 1 July 1974, *Taylor* v. *Taylor*. We quote from page 16 of the court transcript.

> There is one other matter which is that it is to be recorded that the father is to have complete say and control over any inoculations, injection or blood transfusion – and he alone is the parent to consent or refuse consent. The mother is not to be entitled to refuse consent.

The general restrictions that this judgement places on the mother concerning meetings, etc. can be found at the end of the next chapter on children.

The Liberal Elder

The latter end of 1997 saw some very interesting articles appear on the World Wide Web. Elders of the WBTS, who had concluded that the refusing of blood transfusions was wrong both morally and scripturally, put *The Liberal Elder* pages there. The group is determined to get the Governing Body of Jehovah's Witnesses to change its stance on blood and is even willing to take the case to Law.

The pages began with the following explanation,

> Clearly, as Jehovah's Witnesses the Biblical perspective is the paramount issue. Just how compelling of a case can be presented for a scriptural injunction regarding the use of blood? The word 'blood' occurs 540 times in the Bible. It is not practical nor necessary for us to review every verse where this word occurs. We will instead focus attention on those texts that have been used in support of the doctrine, as well as a few other relevant verses that appear relevant. We will attempt to be brief and focus

attention on the most relevant points. We have by no means endeavoured to be exhaustive.

Bible alone

Looking at the Bible in one hand without Watchtower publications in the other hand is very rare. What is interesting to note is that the outcome, as here, is always to reach a view that differs from that of the organisation.

The pages that follow take an in-depth look at many Bible verses and the writings of the early church fathers to show clearly that, whatever the Watchtower says, neither the Bible nor early church history bans blood transfusions. In the middle of another section that traces the history of the ban, we find this interesting statement,

> A key to the development of the current blood doctrine was the appointment of Clayton J. Woodworth as editor of the *Golden Age Magazine*. As we have already learned in the section on Quack Medicine, Br. Woodworth used the magazine as a voice to air his extraordinary personal views on science and medicine. It is here amidst the lunacy and paranoia we find the seeds of the Society's blood doctrine.

Clayton J. Woodworth

Clayton J. Woodworth was co-author of *The Finished Mystery* and in 1919 became editor of the *Golden Age* magazine, a forerunner of today's *Awake!*. He was a supporter of some very strange medical ideas that he propounded regularly in the *Golden Age*. One, more serious, conclusion was that all medical doctors were the agents of Satan.

> We do well to bear in mind that among the drugs, serums, vaccines, surgical operations, etc., of the medical profession, there is nothing of value save an occasional surgical procedure ... Readers of the *Golden Age* know

the unpleasant truth about the clergy; they should also know the truth about the medical profession, which sprang from the same demon worshipping shamans (doctor priests) as did the 'doctors of divinity.' (*Golden Age*, 5 August 1931, pp. 727-728)

The Liberal Elder pages tell us,

Disease, they claimed, came from 'wrong vibrations,' and the WBTS even marketed a special machine called the Electronic Radio Biola, which claimed to heal patients by sending special 'radio waves' ... The claim that the medical profession had descended from 'demon worshipping shamans' becomes quite ironic when we see how this Radio Biola worked: The patient was told to write his or her name on a piece of paper. A tiny piece, only a dot, of this paper with ink was put into the machine. The machine (or rather, the operator) then somehow answered 'yes' and 'no' to questions about the patient's health, reading the 'electronic oscillations' of the patient's organs based on this dot of ink. It was not limited to diagnosis; the machine had even been employed to answer questions about people's life expectancy. If the reader thinks this sounds like a fancy Ouija Board, he is quite correct. One Roy Goodrich, who was such a respected 'Bible Student' that he was allowed to write a warning-article in the *Golden Age*, was convinced this machine was a clever spiritistic trap. The WBTS leadership disagreed, and Mr. Goodrich found himself disfellowshipped. (see *Golden Age*, 22 April 1925, pp. 606-7 and 5 March 1930, pp. 355-62)

Through the 1920's one of Woodworth's major gripes concerned vaccinations; they were 'a crime' and sometimes likened to a rape' as blood transfusions may be today. *The Liberal Elder* concludes that,

Woodworth's primary argument against vaccinations seems to have been that this was 'animal filth' that would 'pollute' humanity. According to the *Golden Age*, vaccinations not only caused all kind of dreadful diseases, including the Spanish Flu, it even retarded the intellect of men and caused moral bankruptcy ... We find these same arguments applied to organ transplants and blood transfusions later!

Blood transfusions themselves were not an issue at this time. It was not until the 1940's that the Society explicitly condemned blood transfusions and then it used the same arguments it had earlier used to ban vaccinations; the arguments that had been laid down by the eccentric views of Clayton Woodworth.

Reform on blood?
In late 1997, Reachout Trust received this e-mail (edited for space reasons) from 'The Associated Jehovah's Witnesses for Reform on Blood'.

> We are a group of elders and Hospital Liaison Committee members in different places and countries. We are very pleased that much good has been accomplished on behalf of our brothers. It is widely acknowledged, even by doctors, that blood is a dangerous medical treatment. Many positive things can be said regarding alternative non-blood therapies, there is no denying that. At the same time, the facts are that our work would not be necessary if medical science were to find a replacement for blood. However, at this time, blood is still a valuable product for saving lives.
>
> A serious question is: What is blood? There are a number of blood components that the Society permits. Are these components not also blood, and how is it decided which parts are acceptable, and which are not? Since it is acceptable to introduce these 'allowed components' into

our bodies, it is understandable that Witnesses and medical personnel are confused by our position.

Albumin is another problem. We accept albumin as a matter of conscience, although the blood contains more albumin than white blood cells, which we must reject. Many doctors are also confused by this position, but what doctors don't know, and we are not permitted to explain to them, is that this position is clearly an organisational ruling for the members, and lacks any logical reason or scriptural support.

For those who have spent some time studying the Society's position on the use of blood, one of the most troubling aspects is their allowance of all of the various components of fresh frozen plasma with the exception of water.

The most depressing feature of being a member of a HLC is when our children are involved. Why has the Society completely failed to gain one legal case when it comes to minor children? It is obvious, there is nothing so effective as human blood to transport oxygen and today there is nothing to replace its use in the medical field. We must appreciate the fact that the legal system protects our children. Even for us, as members of HLC's, we realise that it is much easier to work with the doctors knowing the rules and laws about minor children.

Who is qualified to make a decision about alternative non-blood management, and will that decision adequately meet or respond to the child's needs? As members of the HLC's we have seen cases where co-operative doctors have followed the parent's wishes for alternative non-blood therapy, and the results have sometimes been tragic, with the result of one more unnecessary death.

When we as Jehovah's Witnesses look back and remember the wounded and dead brothers who did not accept vaccinations, blood serums, organ transplants or haemophilic treatments, we must acknowledge that they took their stand largely because of an organisational policy and prohibition forced upon them. These positions have now been abandoned by the leadership, and we rarely if ever see brothers refusing vaccinations, organ transplants, or any of the blood components on the Society's approved list.

Is the Society's blood doctrine actually correct? Why do so many brothers enter into an inner conflict about the issue when they consider the biblical facts? Has the Society really provided us with the truth, and all of the Biblical facts regarding blood? Where are the serious and solid arguments against stored autologous blood transfusions? Should our main concern be to look for medical alternatives, or to discover the biblical facts about life and blood?

We have addressed our concerns to branch representatives and members of the Governing Body. No responses have been forthcoming. If this matter were not so serious, surely we could wait on Jehovah to correct matters in his time. Sadly, we believe that change is being held up because the Society's legal department fears a backlash of litigation from Witnesses who have lost loved ones over this issue.

Our position on blood is in error. For some of us, a measure of bloodguilt may have been incurred in the discharging of our responsibilities. If this is the case, we can hope that Jehovah will be willing to forgive our acts of ignorance. We urge you to get the facts, and prayerfully consider what course of action is appropriate. Some of the questions the Society will not answer:

Why is it that plasma is forbidden when all of its separate components, with the exception of water, are on the approved list for Witnesses to take in order to 'sustain life?'

If a blood transfusion is essentially an organ transplant, how can it be viewed as 'eating blood,' since no digestion or nutritional benefit accrues? Can it be an organ transplant and a meal at the same time?

If storing your own blood for an autologous transfusion is wrong, then why does the Society permit the use of various blood components that must be donated and stored before being used by Jehovah's Witnesses?

How does the Society go about deciding which blood components are major and which are minor? For example, why are white blood cells forbidden, but albumin allowed, since albumin constitutes a larger percentage of blood volume, and milk and organ transplants are full of white blood cells?

If we must abstain from blood completely, as the Society says, then please explain why the Society tells us that we may accept derivatives or components of human blood? Is this not contradictory?

Why can Witnesses accept and benefit from the blood that others donate, but not donate blood themselves? Is this not selfish and hypocritical? Would not giving blood to help save others lives be the loving and Christian thing to do?

Attitude

One phrase in the above e-mail seems to reveal the inner workings of a Witness.

'If this matter were not so serious, surely we could wait on Jehovah to correct matters in his time.'

Note what this means.

1. Jehovah is not able to communicate properly with His 'only channel.'
2. Jehovah needs help in sorting out the problems of His organisation.
3. Although the Society is wrong on such a major point, the Liberal Elder still wants to stay and get the organisation put right.

In May 1998 the Liberal Elder stepped up the campaign for legal action against the WBTS because they feel that 'internal pressure alone will likely be insufficient to bring about reform of the society's blood doctrine.'

They go on to say,

> It is our belief that the continued efforts of the reformers coupled with external pressure in the form of litigation may well be the combination needed to end the needless suffering and death. There is some historical precedent in this regard as the following quotation demonstrates: The matter of vaccination is one for the individual that has to face it to decide for himself. Each individual has to take the consequences for whatever position and action he takes toward a case of compulsory vaccination, doing so according to his own conscience and his appreciation of what is for good health and the interests of advancing God's work. And our Society cannot afford to be drawn into the affair legally or take the responsibility for the way the case turns out.

They desire to produce a legal argument that can be used against the WBTS and proceed with such an action in the United States and other countries.

They believe,

> The issues involved in this case will likely include federal question jurisdiction, invasion of privacy, violations of civil rights, deceptive practices and the involvement of governmental agencies in supporting or otherwise condoning the misconduct of the 'non-profit' corporations of the Watchtower Society, as well as the members of the Governing Body and their assistants.

The matter is very complex and the group is endeavouring to construct a legal team with some experience in litigating these types of cases. What the outcome will be is not yet clear but you can read the latest information at present on Web address http://www.visiworld.com/starter/newlight/index.htm.

The Bulgarian ruling

The Watchtower has also received a jolt from another direction and has had to make blood transfusions a matter of choice! In a legally binding document it agreed to allow free choice on blood transfusions for Jehovah's Witnesses and their children, without any penalties for the choice to take blood.

This historic undertaking was sealed at the 276th Session of the European Commission of Human Rights (Council of Europe) held at the Human Rights Building in Strasbourg from 2 to 13 March 1998. These findings can be confirmed on the European Commission on Human Rights website, http://www.dhcommhr.coe.fr/.

We asked MEP David Hallam what were the legal ramifications of this agreement. Part of his answer in a letter dated 24 September 1998 is as follows:

> ... under the current system, if either side claims that the other has broken the Agreement, the case is then referred to the European Court of Human Rights and Fundamental Freedoms. Both parties are legally bound to adhere to the decision of the Court. However, this system will be changed from 2 November 1998 ... the European Commission on Human Rights will be abolished ... the agreemen t... will however stand; any alleged violation of it would result in automatic and presumably, fast track Court appearance.

The case in question was Khristiansko Sdruzhenie 'Svideteli na Iehova' (Christian Association 'Jehovah's Witnesses') v. Bulgaria (Application No. 28626/95). It concerned Bulgaria's refusal to re-register the applicant association following a 1994 law, and the alleged suppression of its activities and those of its members.

In settlement, the Bulgarian Government agreed to introduce legislation as soon as possible to provide for civilian service as an alternative to military service for conscientious objectors, and to register the applicant association as a religion. The applicant undertook, concerning its stance on blood transfusions, to draft a statement for inclusion in its statute providing that members should have free choice in the matter for themselves and their children, without any control or sanction on the part of the association.

If the Watchtower is to keep its promise to the European Commission, it must officially revoke the instructions found in *WT*, 15 January 1961, p. 64.

> The receiver of a blood transfusion must be cut off from God's people by excommunication or disfellowshiping ... if in the future he persists in accepting blood transfusions or in donating blood toward the carrying out of this medical practice upon others, he shows that he has really not repented, but is deliberately opposed to God's requirements. As a rebellious opposer and unfaithful example to fellow members of the Christian congregation he must be cut off therefrom by disfellowshiping.

It will be interesting to see what the results of these challenges will be to Watchtower policy. What is evident is that it is up to its old tricks of denying its members the full information and indeed twisting the truth of a legal ruling.

The quote from the European Commission of Human Rights is clear, 'The applicant undertook concerning its stance on BLOOD TRANSFUSIONS to draft a statement for inclusion in its statute providing that members should have free choice in the matter for themselves and their children, without any control or sanction on the part of the association.'

However, the press release put out by the Society says in part,

The European Commission of Human Rights decided to accept the amicable settlement agreed to by the Government of Bulgaria and the Christian Association of Jehovah's Witnesses ... Bulgaria has agreed to grant the Christian Association of Jehovah's Witnesses recognition as a religion. Bulgaria also agreed to create without delay a bill that will allow alternative civilian service for those whose conscience will not allow them to engage in military service. The agreement also includes an acknowledgement that each individual has the freedom to choose the type of MEDICAL TREATMENT he receives. With the amicable settlement, the Witnesses agreed to withdraw their complaint against Bulgaria.

What other aspects of medical treatment could there be? How can this be the only organisation that God is using today when it employs such deceptive methods to keep its own people in the dark? It will only be its own members that do not find out the truth because they will accept the Watchtower press release and not check the original. I have had an interesting exchange of e-mails with one such Jehovah's Witness. 'The Watchtower press release is right and all other documentation wrong.' All we can do is plead with such people that they investigate and discover the truth for themselves.

NOTE 1

The accusation that numerous children of Jehovah's Witnesses die each year as a result of refusing blood transfusions is totally unfounded. (*WT*, 1 December 1998, p. 14)

This was not what the Society was saying in 1994 when they highlighted the story of two youths, one 14 and one 12, who died through lack of a blood transfusion. The WBTS commented:

By rejecting blood transfusions that could conceivably have extended his present life, Adrian Yeatts showed himself to be ONE OF THE MANY YOUNG PEOPLE who put God first. (*Aw.*, 22 May 1994, p. 8)

14

Social issues – children

— ❧ —

It can be a shock to find an adult on your doorstep with a very young child who appears to be able to recite the 'Witness patter' very well. It can be an even greater shock to find two young children together. Reachout Trust receives an increasing number of calls enquiring about the position of the Society regarding children. Usually these are to do with custody cases going through the courts.

As we will show in the next chapter on 'disfellowshipping,' children will suffer emotional hardships in the break up of families. But what of the child who is put with the Witness partner in a custody case, or even a Witness child in a united family; are wrong pressures placed on them?

We have been asked to provide information in a number of cases. The courts are reluctant to take the children away from their mother unless there is ample evidence of inability to look after them. What has happened in some cases though is that the court order includes restrictions on the child's attendance at the Kingdom Hall and the door-to-door work as well as giving joint custody on medical matters such as blood transfusions.

The Watchtower is aware of the increasing number of court cases. We mentioned the letter sent to solicitors in chapter 13. The second area it was looking to cover was these court cases and reads:

The other area involves disputes over residence of and contact with children. Here the question of religious beliefs and the associated refusal of homologous blood are often allowed to assume totally disproportionate significance ... we are looking for specialists in child-care litigation who can provide our members with skilled, sympathetic advice. We would also be keen to know if your firm has had any experience in handling such cases for Jehovah's Witnesses.

Its concern has gone as far as producing an internal booklet to help its members in such cases entitled *Preparing For Child Custody Cases*. This coaches the Witness in what sort of questions they will be asked and what responses they should give.

Duane Magnani, who runs Witness Inc., a ministry in California to help Jehovah's Witnesses has produced *Refutation of 'Preparing for Child Custody Cases'*. This points to various Watchtower publications that show exactly what Witnesses believe and can be produced in court as evidence if needed. Any who may be involved in such cases need to obtain a copy of this book from Reachout Trust.

In it we see that the Witness is told to lie about what they actually believe or, if not lie, certainly to hide the truth. For instance when talking about blood transfusions Witnesses are told 'You do not want to give the impression that your religion requires you to allow your child to die should a medical emergency arise.' (*Preparing for Child Custody Cases*, WBTS, 1988, p. 55) Nevertheless, in some circumstances that is exactly what their religion requires them to do.

When several young people may be brought before the court to show that they are normal and healthy, they are warned, when asked about future plans, 'Be careful they don't all say that they are going to be pioneers.' (*Preparing for Child Custody Cases*, WBTS, 1988, p. 43) But that is exactly what they are regularly exhorted to be in the Society's publications and talks at the Kingdom Hall.

These are just two examples of what Witnesses are taught not to do. But it will also be helpful for us to see what children are taught to do. Just what instruction do they and their parents receive from the Watchtower?

Who can children associate with?

It would follow, then, that *any recreation* you take outside of SCHOOL SHOULD NOT BE WITH WORLDLY YOUTHS ... (*WT*, 1 September 1964, p. 535)

The ideal situation is for parents to have such a fine program outlined for their children that LITTLE OR NO TIME REMAINS FOR OUTSIDE ASSOCIATION. (*WT*, 1 February 1974, p. 93)

To keep separate from the world while in school, young Witnesses should consider THE DANGERS OF BECOMING INVOLVED IN EXTRA-CURRICULUAR ACTIVITIES. (*Organized to Accomplish Our Ministry*, 1983, p. 133)

So Witness parents encourage their children to use after-school hours principally to pursue spiritual interests, rather than to excel in some sport. Participation in organized sports, we believe, would expose Witness youths to UNWHOLESOME ASSOCIATIONS. (*School and Jehovah's Witnesses*, 1983, p. 23)

Which recreations are banned?

Much time is wasted that could be better spent in learning profitable matters or in preaching activity. SPORTS AS ORGANIZED TODAY are conducive to hero worship, which is dangerous and unchristian. (*WT*, 15 January 1952, p. 46)

The extreme fascination of CHESS can result in its consuming large amounts of one's time ... even developing hostility toward another ... (*Aw.*, 22 March 1973, p. 14)

And do you show empathy when you imprison us in your zoos in restricting cages to be gawked at? How do you think we feel? Would you like to change places with us? (*Aw.*, 8 May 1973, p. 18)

Children in service

Do you engage in field service regularly, TAKING YOUR CHILDREN along? Do they observe you in door-to-door work; back-call work and home Bible study work, hearing you make effective presentations? (*WT*, 15 January 1954, pp. 50-51)

Parents who love their children and who want TO SEE THEM ALIVE in God's new world will encourage and guide them toward goals of increased service and responsibility. (*WT*, 15 March 1962, p. 179)

Activity in the Christian ministry cannot be confined to adults. It is a privilege of service that you children can Scripturally participate in and SHOULD ENGAGE IN. If you want to obey Jehovah you will ENGAGE REGULARLY ... serve your Creator EVERY DAY during vacation periods ... do you obey him by ZEALOUSLY ENGAGING IN IT REGULARLY? (*WT*, 15 August 1962, p. 493)

Be a regular publisher by sharing in the field ministry. Then when SECULAR SCHOOL IS OUT, BE A VACATION PIONEER ... with the goal of later entering into the full-time service as a PERMANENT CAREER. (*Qualified To Be Ministers*, 1967, p. 258)

Children should be trained at a VERY EARLY AGE to accompany their parents in the field Ministry. (*Our Kingdom Ministry*, June 1982, p. 4)

Loyalty to Jehovah and his organization is necessary if we are to gain everlasting life. At this time of testing, how can Christian youths maintain integrity? ... Increasing numbers of young ones are rejecting high-paying jobs or higher education in favor of a CAREER IN THE MINISTRY. They humbly accept counsel and direction from older ones that will ENABLE THEM TO CONTINUE IN LOYAL SACRED SERVICE. (*Our Kingdom Ministry*, August 1982, pp. 1, 3)

It would hardly be consistent for such a youth, of his own choice, to pursue EXTENSIVE SECULAR STUDIES beyond what is REQUIRED BY THE LAW OR BY HIS PARENTS. (*WT*, 1 September 1975, p. 543)

However, as the Society has became more automated it found it lacked necessary skills amongst Witnesses. But it was the parents who had second thoughts, not the Watchtower.

It is no shame for a person to learn a trade and work with his hands. Indeed, these days it is getting to be the practical thing to do. That is another reason why SOME PARENTS now have second thoughts about the matter of a college education. (*Aw.*, 8 June 1971, p. 8)

Pressure!

ALL MEMBERS OF THE FAMILY ... should be interested in furthering pioneer activity and willing to make sacrifices to that end. (*WT*, 15 March 1975, p. 187)

If you would like to get to KNOW YOUR CHILDREN BETTER, what they are really thinking ... ascertaining how much they really love Jehovah, ARRANGE TIME TO TAKE THEM WITH YOU IN THE FIELD SERVICE. (*Our Kingdom Service*, June 1976, p. 4)

Are you young publishers showing a willingness to study with your parents and accompany them in the field service? You can be sure Jehovah is pleased with you when

you do. Yes, both PARENTS AND CHILDREN ARE CALLED UPON TO
SHOW APPRECIATION FOR THE FAMILY ARRANGEMENT. (*Our
Kingdom Service*, December 1977, p. 4)

Parents, of course, have the ADDITIONAL RESPONSIBILITY of
helping their children to be ACTIVE in spiritual things ...
WORK OUT A REASONABLE SCHEDULE of theocratic activity ...
Thus, they show a personal interest in their CHILDREN'S
WELFARE. .. (Our Kingdom Ministry, December 1982, p. 2)

Being used

Children can often create a favourable impression in the
minds of householders who have not shown much interest in the Bible. (*YB* 1964, p. 161)

She [a four-year old] is my help during times of opposition. When I find a householder opposing I ask my
daughter to give the sermon. (*YB*, 1965, p. 223)

Adult publishers are often glad to have young ministers
along ... Sometimes people will not open their doors to
a man alone ... but will be inclined to ... listen when a
youngster publisher is along. (*Kingdom Ministry*, October
1972, p. 3)

Children are often the center of attention ... Some
casual statement or incident might prompt the children
to speak up in an appealing way that touches the heart
of other family members. (*Our Kingdom Ministry*,
December 1983, p. 4)

Correction and disfellowshipping

In the case of where a father or mother or son or daughter is disfellowshiped, how should such a person be
treated by members of the family ... The parent must by
laws of God and of man fulfil his parental obligations to

the child or children as long as they are dependent minors, and the child or children must render filial submission to the parent as long as legally underage ... Of course, if the children are of age, then there can be a departing and BREAKING OF FAMILY TIES ... If children are of age and continue to associate with a disfellowshiped parent because of receiving material support ... they must consider how far their spiritual interests are being endangered ... and whether they can arrange to support themselves, LIVING APART FROM THE FALLEN-AWAY PARENT. (*WT*, November 1952, p. 703)

A baptized child's being a minor does not shield him from REPROOF BEFORE THE CONGREGATION by the elders, or DISFELLOWSHIPING, if he commits serious wrongdoing. (*Organization for Kingdom-Preaching and Disciple-Making*, 1972, p. 175)

A few years ago, a Witness whose daughter decided to stop studying at thirteen and go 'into the world' contacted us. The mother was encouraged to either get her to change or to leave home and the latter happened. Tragically the daughter tried to commit suicide a little while later, but fortunately did not succeed. Now the mother is faced with the dilemma of loving and helping the daughter or obeying the Society.

Are your children in danger?

If, for example, a fifteen-year-old boy answers the door, what is your reaction? ... has the boy ever heard the good news of the Kingdom ... most young people these days have a little money and it may be possible to place a ... book ... (*Kingdom Ministry*, February 1973, p. 8)

We should not feel that we must always ask to speak to their parents ... Where can we find young people? ... search them out ... at summer camps, in the vicinity of summer schools or in recreational areas. (*Our Kingdom Service*, August 1977, p. 4)

Concern of the courts for children

We are not saying that most or indeed many Witness mothers or fathers are terrible parents. Most care deeply for their children but feel that they need to put Jehovah first. In the case we have already quoted (*Taylor* v *Taylor*, Royal Courts of Justice, Monday 1 July 1974) there was no criticism of the mother in the care for the child. However because of her behaviour the judge felt that the children were 'being indoctrinated as Jehovah's Witnesses'. (p. 13)

Because of this he ruled:

> However, there are going to be a number of conditions attached to the mother's care and control ... The children are to be with the father at Christmas time ... There must be no restriction upon their taking part in school assembly or in any Christmas or other play. Subject to being at school, they must spend their birthdays with their father, and if they cannot spend the actual day then he is able to celebrate their birthdays with them on the next access. There will be a complete prohibition against the mother taking them out witnessing, that is, going around from door to door or taking them with her when she is engaged on the external business of Jehovah's Witnesses. They are not to be taken to Jehovah's Witness conventions or meetings of any kind, other than the hall meeting on a Sunday.

This obviously indicates the concern that some judges have over children heavily influenced by one Jehovah's Witness parent.

15

Social issues – disfellowshipping

— ☙ —

Disfellowshipping is the excommunicating of a member of the WBTS because they do not 'toe the line.' For a Witness this means that not only will they have problems to face here on earth but also they will have no hope of any form of eternal life. This is the result of equating the membership of the Society with the only hope of salvation. (We use the British spelling of 'disfellowshipping' with 'pp'. Quotes from modern Watchtower literature use 'p'.)

It is true that the Bible does advocate a form of separation for people who deliberately and wilfully go against God's commands. Sadly, it may also be true that some churches have failed to heed this Bible counsel whereas the Watchtower take it too far in its application of these sound biblical principles.

The biblical purpose of disfellowshipping is to cause the errant Christian to repent, to remove what could be a stumbling block from the church, so that others will not be affected, to teach others to fear God's righteous judgement and to keep the church clean in the eyes of outsiders. In 1 Cor. 5 we read of Paul's instructions to remove a Christian who was cohabiting with his stepmother. However, it is possible that this is the man who would become 'overwhelmed by excessive sorrow' and later Paul encourages the church to 'reaffirm your love for him' (see 2 Cor. 2:6-11). Unruly Christians who would not respond to counselling were to be treated similarly, as 2 Thess. 3:14-15 shows. Verse 15 is particularly relevant to the Watchtower.

In Matt. 18:15-18 Jesus Christ outlines three steps to take in settling difficulties, or righting the wrong. If the steps proved unsuccessful then the person was to be treated as a 'Gentile and a tax-gatherer' (Matt. 18:17b). Yet, despite the Jews' hatred for Gentiles and tax-gatherers they still had cause to deal with them from time to time. In all this we should also remember the heart of the Lord that He 'is not willing for any to perish but for all to come to repentance' (2 Pet 3:9). So, the object of disfellowshipping should always include trying to persuade the sinner to have a repentant attitude and return to the Lord.

The Watchtower has gone further than the practice of disfellowshipping unrepentant sinners, and has included in its reasons for disfellowshipping smoking, working for military establishments, working for other religious organisations, voting in elections, accepting blood transfusions and celebrating birthdays or holidays such as Christmas and Easter. Talking to other disfellowshipped ones, even if they are a relative counts as a reason. In addition, if a dissatisfied person disagrees with Watchtower teaching and discusses that disagreement with other Jehovah's Witnesses to promote apostasy, then that person will be disfellowshipped. Thus the organisation protects itself from general discontentment and enforces unity by use of disfellowshipping.

The Society has instilled into its membership an attitude of fear, teaching that its 'organisation' is God's organisation and that to turn away from it is the same as turning away from God Himself. The Governing Body, frightened that members will communicate with ex-members and find out the truth, forbids such communication with ex-members. Tremendous difficulties arise within family relationships because of this hard attitude.

The Watchtower's stance
The Watchtower has not always maintained this strong position.

1920   'We would not refuse to treat one as a brother because he did not believe the Society is the Lord's channel.' (*WT*, 1 April, p. 100)

1930s	However, the Society did not take long to change its views. By 1930 those who disagreed with President Rutherford were classed as 'evil slaves' and were called the 'man of perdition' who would be destroyed. In more recent times though its position on disfellowshipping has been solidified.
1952	Disfellowshipping was discussed fully and the conclusion concerning a disfellowshipped person was that 'Those who are acquainted with the situation in the congregation should never say "Hello" or "Good-by" to him. He is not welcome in our midst, we avoid him.' (*WT*, 1 March, pp. 137-45)
1955	Associating with a disfellowshipped person can now lead to an active Jehovah's Witness being disfellowshipped. (*WT*, 1 October, p. 607)
1974	Disfellowshipped ones are not to be treated with unnecessary cruelty, especially members of a Witnesses' own family or house in obvious hardship situations. They should not be like the Pharisees who walked on the other side of the road. (*WT*, 1 August, pp. 466-73)
1981	New hard lines are to be taken with those disfellowshipped, or those who leave, called 'disassociated'. Even family members are to be shunned except in the most necessary functions of life. (*WT*, 15 September, pp. 20-31)
1985	Any who abandon the organisation are part of the 'antichrist' and 2 John 9-11 applies to them. They should not even be greeted. (*WT*, 15 July, pp. 30-31)

The results of disfellowshipping

We can also trace the history of a number of other aspects of disfellowshipping.

Hate

Haters of God and his people are to be hated ... We must hate in the truest sense, which is to regard with extreme and active aversion, to consider as loathsome, odious, filthy, to detest. Surely any HATERS OF GOD are not fit to live on his beautiful earth ... What do you do with anything loathsome ...? The answer is simple. You get away from it or remove it from your presence. You do not want to have anything at all to do with it. This must be exactly our attitude towards the haters of Jehovah ... (*WT*, 1 October 1952, p. 599)

When a person persists in a way of badness after knowing what is right, when the bad becomes so ingrained that it is an inseparable part of his make-up then in order to hate what is bad a CHRISTIAN MUST HATE the person with whom the badness is inseparably linked. (*WT*, 15 July 1961, p. 420)

So it is that ENLIGHTENED CHRISTIANS RIGHTLY HATE those who are confirmed enemies of God, such as the Devil and his demons, as well as MEN who have deliberately and knowingly taken their stand against Jehovah. (*WT*, 15 November 1970, p. 695)

When we realise that any who merely question consistently the Watchtower organisation are considered as rebelling against God Himself, the above words of hatred take on a sinister aspect.

Against the 'Organisation' means against God

Against whom was this rebellion directed? Against certain individuals in authority in the church ... But the rebellion was actually against God ... When anyone takes an unfaithful course, challenging Jehovah's word or arrangement, he is ranging himself up against God. (*WT*, 15 March 1975, p. 167)

Thus, the one who doubts to the point of becoming apostate sets himself up as a judge. He thinks he knows better ... than the 'faithful and discreet slave' ... He develops a spirit of independence ... Some apostates even think they know better than God, as regards his ordering of events and outworking of his purposes. (*WT*, 1 August 1980, pp. 19-20)

Renouncing your Christian standing
A person who says he no longer wants to be known as a Jehovah's Witness is said to be renouncing his standing as a Christian.

One who has been a true Christian might renounce the way of the truth, stating that he no longer considers himself to be one of Jehovah's Witnesses or wants to be one. When this rare event occurs, the person is renouncing his standing as a Christian ... (*WT*, 15 September 1981, p. 23)

The wrongdoing of leaving the organisation
Persons who make themselves 'not of our sort' by deliberately rejecting the faith and beliefs of Jehovah's Witnesses should appropriately be viewed and treated as are those who have been disfellowshiped for wrongdoing. (*WT*, 15 September 1981, p. 23)

The fact is that when a Christian gives himself over to sin and has to be disfellowshiped, he forfeits ... his approved standing with God ... much of the association he had with Christian relatives. (*WT*, 15 September 1981, p. 31)

How to view a disfellowshipped relative

A disfellowshiped person has been SPIRITUALLY cut off from the congregation; the former spiritual ties have been completely severed. This is true even with respect to his relatives, including those within the immediate family circle. Thus, family members – while acknowledging family ties – will no longer have any spiritual fellowship with him. (*WT*, 15 September 1981, p. 28)

Prayer or Bible study

If he [a disfellowshipped husband] wants to say a prayer, such as at mealtimes, he has a right to do so in his own home. But they [the Witness relatives] can silently offer their own prayers to God ... What if a disfellowshiped person in the home wants to be present when the family read the Bible together or has a Bible Study? The others might let him be present to listen if he will not try to teach them or share his religious ideas. (*WT*, 15 September 1981, p. 28)

The disfellowshipped parent or child who lives away from home

For example, a disfellowshiped parent may be sick or no longer able to care for himself financially or physically. The Christian children have a Scriptural and moral obligation to assist ... Perhaps it seems necessary to bring the parent into the home ... What is done may depend on factors such as the parent's true needs, his attitude and the regard the head of the household has for the spiritual welfare of the household. This could also be true with regard to a child who had left home but is now disfellowshiped or disassociated. Sometimes Christian parents have accepted back into the home for a time a disfellowshiped child ... But in each case the parents can weigh the individual circumstances ... What about his morals and attitude? Will he bring 'leaven' into the home? (*WT*, 15 September 1981, pp. 28-29)

The Society is laying down rules as to how to treat one's own parents or children but it uses such terms as 'moral obligation,' not love. Surely a very cold way of looking at things.

Family events

Normally, relatives are often together at meals, picnics, family reunions or other social gatherings. But when someone has unrepentantly pursued sin and has had to be disfellowshiped, he may cause difficulties for his Christian relatives in regard to such gatherings. (*WT*, 15 September 1981, p. 30)

Weddings and receptions

It should be appreciated that if a disfellowshiped person is going to be at a gathering to which non-relative Witnesses are invited, that may well affect what others do. For example, a Christian couple might get married at a Kingdom Hall. If a disfellowshiped relative comes to the Kingdom Hall for the wedding, obviously he could not be in the bridal party there or 'give away' the bride. What, though, if there is a wedding feast or reception? This can be a happy social occasion, as it was in Cana when Jesus attended. But will the disfellowshiped relative be allowed to come or even invited? If he was going to attend, many Christians, relatives or not, might conclude that they should not be there, to eat and associate with him, in view of Paul's directions at 1 Cor. 5:11. Thus, sometimes Christians may not feel able to have a disfellowshiped or disassociated relative present for a gathering that normally would include family members. (*WT*, 15 September 1981, p. 30)

Funeral arrangements

The instructions of the Society extend even after death.

> Should he die while disfellowshiped, arrangements for his funeral may be a problem. His Christian relatives may like to have had a talk at the Kingdom Hall ... But that would not be fitting for a person expelled from the congregation. If he had been giving evidence of repentance ... such as by ... attending Christian meetings, some brother's conscience might allow him to have a Bible talk at the funeral home or grave site ... However, if the disfellowshiped person had still been advocating false teachings or ungodly conduct, even such a talk would not be appropriate. (*WT*, 15 September 1981, p. 31)

Attitude of relatives not living with the disfellowshipped one

> The second situation we need to consider is that involving a disfellowshiped or disassociated relative who is not in the immediate family circle or living at one's home ... Consequently, Christians related to such a disfellowshiped person living outside the home should strive to avoid needless association, even keeping business dealings to a minimum. (*WT*, 15 September 1981, p. 29)

> The disfellowshiping of a relative does not cancel out natural blood ties. However, it would be well to appreciate that only the contacts absolutely necessary in matters pertaining to family interests should be carried on ... In the case of the disfellowshiped relative who does not live in the same home, contact with him is also kept to what is absolutely necessary. As with secular employment, this contact is limited and even curtailed completely if at all possible ... If courtesies are extended, though, the Christian should make it clear that this will not be a reg-

ular practice ... The excommunicated relative should be made to realize that his visits are not now welcomed as they were previously when he was walking correctly with Jehovah ... If all family ties with an excommunicated person were kept as before, in what way could it be said that the brothers were co-operating with the disfellowshiping procedure, which is designed to keep God's visible organization clean? ... Bible principles do not support regular association with relatives who do not live in the same home with a disfellowshiped person... We should not see how close we can get to relatives who are disfellowshiped from Jehovah's organization, but we should 'quit mixing in company' with them. (*WT*, 15 July 1963, pp. 443-44)

But the disfellowshiped relative should be made to appreciate that his status has changed, that he is no longer welcome in the home nor is he a preferred companion... He (God) also instructs Christians 'never to receive him into their home or say a greeting to him'. If normal social communion between relatives were maintained with this disfellowshiped one, a thing that is not necessary since he lives outside the home, would the Christian be obeying God? ... We must keep in clear focus the fact that the disfellowshiped one's not being able to enjoy the companionship of his Christian relatives is not their fault, as if they were treating him shoddily. They are acting according to ... God's principles. The disfellowshiped one himself is responsible for his situation; he has brought it upon himself. Let the burden rest where it belongs ... A disfellowshiped person who is repentant can be forgiven and reinstated into the congregation ... But until that happens, faithful Christians have an obligation to uphold the disfellowshiping action by avoiding association with the disfellowshiped individual. If that one is a relative living outside the home, they will try to have no fellowship with him at all. (*WT*, 1 June 1970, p. 352)

Say 'Hello' and you may be disfellowshipped

As distinct from some personal 'enemy' or worldly man in authority who opposes Christians, a disfellowshiped or disassociated person who is trying to promote or justify his apostate thinking or is continuing in his ungodly conduct is certainly not one to whom to wish 'Peace' ... And we all know from our experience over the years that a simple 'Hello' to someone can be the first step that develops into a conversation and maybe even a friendship. Would we want to take that first step with a disfellowshiped person? ... If the elders saw him heading in that direction by regularly keeping company with a disfellowshiped person, they would lovingly and patiently try to help him to regain God's view ... But if he will not cease to fellowship with the expelled person, he ... must be removed from the congregation, expelled. (*WT*, 15 September 1981, pp. 25-26)

Emotional ties

Naturally, if a close relative is disfellowshiped, human emotions can prove a major test for us. Sentiment and family ties are particularly strong between parents and their children, and they are also powerful when a marriage mate is disfellowshiped. Still we must recognize that, in the final analysis, we will not benefit anyone or please God if we allow emotion to lead us into ignoring His wise counsel and guidance. (*WT*, 15 September 1981, pp. 31)

How many?

The world-wide casualties of this policy of disfellowshipping are, according to the Society's own statistics approximately 100 per day!

Shocking as it is, even some who have been prominent in Jehovah's organization have succumbed to immoral practices, including homosexuality, wife swapping, and child molesting. It is to be noted, also, that during the past year, 36,638 individuals had to be disfellowshiped from the Christian congregation, the GREATER NUMBER of them for practising immorality. (*WT*, 1 January 1986, p. 13)

Conclusion

Can you imagine being in a situation where you are totally rejected, treated as dead? The Watchtower discourages association and friendship with those outside the organisation. So when a person leaves they are treated as a sinner rebelling against God Himself, and not even to be greeted. There is a dramatic change in their family relationship. If all the Watchtower instructions are obeyed, they would hardly, if ever, see their relatives living outside the home and much of the normal family social life would be curtailed or stopped completely.

Under these circumstances, people have tried to commit suicide and families have broken up. Imagine the pressure on the Witness wife of the disfellowshipped one. She still loves her husband yet the instructions of the Society begin to drive a wedge between their loving relationship. Her husband is no longer welcome in the Witness homes she visits.

Think of the person who has left. They were deceived for years by a false prophet and are scared to put their trust in another 'denomination.' They are desperate to experience love and kindness. If such a disfellowshipped one visits your church, are you ready to act with the love and understanding they need?

16

The challenge

___ ୬ ___

Should Christians talk with Jehovah's Witnesses?

There has been much controversy over whether Christians should invite Jehovah's Witnesses into their homes for discussion. In the final analysis, we must each be led by our conscience. However, there is no reason why we cannot talk with them on the doorstep.

Whenever we are talking with a Witness we want to get from A to B. A is what we know of Jesus and salvation, grace and mercy, etc. B is when the Witness has had opportunity to receive this in a loving and relevant way. Of course, it is not always a direct route, the Witness may take you via X, Y & Z. However how many detours you take is not important, nor indeed is how many arguments you loose. What is important is that, in the time you have, you share Jesus in a relevant way.

The Witness may be on their guard, seeing you as the 'enemy', and it will help if you start by lovingly sowing doubt concerning the organisation. Ask difficult questions (See Note 1) because if they open their mind to the possibility that the WBTS may *not* be God's organisation they will be in a much better frame of mind to accept what you are saying. However, if you do not have time to do this just share Jesus because He alone saves, not our good presentations.

There is no point in engaging in 'Wimbledon Witnessing' where you stand on the base line and smash a text down the throat of your opponent. We want to build bridges, not have a tennis match where we may score points but win no trophies!

Ask questions and present the Scriptures as we have in this book. It really is not what you say but it is the way that you say it. Build bridges, not brick walls. The cassette tape *Who's There?* and the video *Reaching out to Jehovah's Witnesses*, both available from Reachout Trust, give practical demonstrations of how this can be done.

Mix and match

In several chapters of this book you will have found 'presentations' that you can use both to sow doubt and to share Jesus. Use the ones that you are comfortable with and do not be afraid to try something new.

New Christians

We believe it is vital that you never go out of your spiritual depth when sharing with a Jehovah's Witness. If you are a new Christian and do not yet know the doctrines of the Christian faith, it is better to take a very simple approach. However, if we are Christians who are well versed we should not use this as an excuse not to talk.

Our suggestion for new Christians is to listen to the opening presentation of the Witness and then turn it around so you can give a personal testimony of Jesus. For instance, you could say 'Thank you for calling and sharing these things with me but I want you to know that I have already made a decision to serve God fully. Let me tell you what happened ... '

Once completed, you can politely excuse yourself or pass them on to someone who can take them further. Of course within a few months you might also be able to present some of the simple Scriptures we list here. Alternatively, after giving your testimony, you could present a simple gospel message using some of these Scriptures.

Jehovah's way of salvation
      John 6:40 –   Look to the Son
      Matt. 17:5 –   Listen to the Son

John 14:21–   Obey the Son
Acts 4:12 –   Only name
John 14:6 –   Through the Son

The reason we go through the Son
John 10:28 –   He gives life
John 5:22 –   He is our Judge
Matt. 11:28 –   He gives rest
John 14:27 –   He gives peace
Col. 2:15 –   He won the victory on the cross
John 5:23–   Therefore we give Him the same honour as the Father

What we must recognise
Rom. 3:23 –   All are sinners
Rom. 3:10ff –   Acknowledge our condition
1 Pet. 2:24 –   Christ took away our sin in His body
Rom. 4:25 –   Christ died in our place
Luke 13:3 –   We must repent or perish
Acts 26:20 –   Our life must fit our repentance

Finally, three Scriptures that sum up the gospel of Jesus Christ well are 1 Cor. 15:3, 1 Cor. 2:2 and Luke 24:46ff.

Preparation

Take time now, having read this book, to be prepared for the next Witness that calls.

- List the information you feel comfortable in sharing that will sow doubt in the Jehovah's Witness.
- Write out, if you need to, the Biblical presentations on *Jesus* and *Salvation* that you would want to use. Study to discover the answers to any difficult verses that you know the Witness might use.

- At all times show patience, courtesy and love, even if it means saying the same thing many times over in different ways.

Proactive

We trust that everyone who has read this book will be ready to talk with the next Witness who calls at their door, however we hope that some will become proactive. There are ways that you can go out and find Witnesses and ways that you can reach out in love to your town and community. If this is something that you feel could be for you please see Appendix C.

After

Appendix A is a Bible Study that has been devised especially for Jehovah's Witnesses who have left the Society or who are thinking of leaving the Society. It leaves them to find the answers from the Scriptures themselves, instead of being told from the publications! You are welcome to photocopy these pages to use in suitable situations.

NOTE 1

You will have found some of these questions in the various chapters but there are others contained in the publications marked **Q** in Appendix B.

ADDITIONAL STUDY

Chapter 4 – The Godhead – Father

Although the Society does not mention the 'P. Ryl. GK. 458' copy it does, in *NWT*, refer to nine other copies (see below – Number 1 is the P. Fouad Inv. No. 266 already mentioned) of the LXX in order to bolster its case, yet only one (Number 5) is dated before Christ, and that does not strictly contain the tetragram. This fact is vital when it is seeking to prove that Jesus would have read and pronounced the tetragram in the synagogue. Only BC manuscripts could prove this. Any written by Jewish scribes after Christ would simply show the desire to keep old traditions. We will look at this evidence to see what the Society's case is.

Number 2 – LXX^VTS10a

Dated the end of first century, the review in *Supplements to Vetus Testamentum* Vol. X, 1963, pp. 170-78, declares it to be a 'recension of the ancient LXX,' that is, it was a revision. It also says that its wording was literal to the Hebrew, thus showing the reason for the revision is to harp back to the old Jewish traditions.

It is helpful here to note F. F. Bruce's explanation as to why there were many Jewish revisions of the LXX harping back to old traditions:

> There were two main reasons why the Jews lost interest in the Septuagint. One was that from the first century AD onwards the Christians adopted it as their version of the Old Testament ... Another reason for the Jew's loss of interest in the Septuagint lies in the fact that about AD 100 a revised standard text was established for the Hebrew Bible by Jewish scholars ... any version in

another language which was to be fit for Jewish use must conform to it. (*The Books and the Parchments*, 1953, pp. 145-46)

Number 3 – LXX[IEJ12]

Dated first century AD, this is recorded in *The Israel Exploration Journal* Vol. 12, 1962, p. 201-07, by B. Lifshitz of the Hebrew University, Jerusalem. This is part of his account:

> Some ten years ago Père D. Barthélemy published a paper in which he made mention of, among other things, fragments of a parchment scroll containing the Greek Translation of the Minor Prophets ... Père Barthélemy concluded that the version of this scroll is neither a new translation nor an independent one, but rather a recension of the Septuagint; and that its variations from the Septuagint are the result of an attempt to render Greek in a manner FAITHFUL TO THE HEBREW ORIGINAL. (p. 201)

The *NWT* only mentions four verses in Zechariah where the tetragram is found. But B. Lifshitz, on p. 204 of the same article, shows an extract from Nahum 1:9 and comments 'This small fragment is too meagre to allow for an attempt at reconstructing the version of the scroll; however, IT IS CLEAR THAT *THEOS* APPEARS instead of *kyrios* of the Septuagint.'

The same is written about Zech. 4:8a and clearly shows the inconsistency of this version in using the tetragram. In both the above places, the NWT has 'Jehovah,' but this particular version does not have the tetragram and therefore must disqualify itself from being reliable evidence on behalf of the Society.

Number 4 – LXX[VTS10b]

The Society has tried to make this a separate case. However, you will notice its catalogue number is very close to Number 2 and indeed the fragments were reviewed in the same article. All that was said about Number 2 applies here.

Number 5 – 4Q LXX Lev^b

Found in the Qumram caves and definitely of Jewish origin, dated first century BC. However, its review in *Supplements to Vetus Testamentum* Vol. IV, 1957, pp. 148-58, puts a different light on this find than the one the Society would have us believe. Two points need to be made. Firstly, this fragment does not have the tetragram but a Greek substitute (*iaw*). The article comments 'Its only special feature is that in the midst of the Greek text, familiar from the LXX codices, the divine name here appears NOT AS *KYRIOS* BUT AS *IAW*.'

What is apparent from this is that the majority of LXX codices contained *kyrios*, not the tetragram, and indeed that this version does not contain the tetragram. The second matter to note is that although Qumram was a bastion of Jewish tradition it did not use the tetragram. The *New International Dictionary of New Testament Theology* informs us 'Members of the Qumram sect, in Heb[rew] biblical MSS [manuscripts], were writing *adonay*, Lord, instead of the tetragrammaton.' (Vol. 2, p. 512)

Number 6 – LXX^{P.Oxy.VII.1007}

Dated third century AD and described by A. S. Hunt in *The Oxyrhynchus Papyri, 1910, Part VII*. Here again the Society decides not to present all the evidence to its readers. Why is this representation of the tetragram there? A. S. Hunt explains:

> ... a most remarkable abbreviation of the so-called Tetragrammaton, WHICH IN THE SEPTUAGINT IS REGULARLY REPRESENTED BY *KYRIOS*. This abbreviation consists of a double Yod, the initial of the sacred name, written in the shape of a Z with a horizontal stroke through the middle ... A DECIDED TENDENCY TO OMIT THE WORD *KYRIOS* was, however, observable in the early Oxyrhynchus papyrus (656),

where in one passage a blank space was originally left in which the missing word was supplied by a second hand (pp. 1-2).

From this, we understand three things about this version:

1. It is a remarkable, not a normal and often used, abbreviation, therefore, it would not be commonly found in the LXX.
2. It was a 'decided tendency' of the Jewish scribe to use this tetragram rather than *kyrios*.
3. A similar and older version 656, containing the end of Gen. 2 and beginning of 3, left a blank space four times. Another scribe later added *theos* or *kyrios* in three of these places.

Numbers 7 and 8 – Aq[Burkitt] and Aq[Taylor]

These are different versions of the same manuscript, translated by Aquila (about AD 100), dated around the fifth or sixth century. But who was Aquila? The WBTS itself says 'Aquila was a Jewish proselyte of Pontus in Asia, AN APOSTATE FROM CHRISTIAN-ITY.' (*Equipped for every Good Work*, WBTS, 1946, p. 52)

We read from other sources:

> What is certain is that he was a pupil of the new rabbinical school ... (his version) was an extraordinary production ... No jot or tittle of the Heb[rew] might be neglected; uniformity in the tr[anslation] of each Heb[rew] word must be preserved ... a bold attempt to displace the LXX. (*International Standard Bible Encyclopaedia*, 1978, Vol. 4, p. 2725)

> Moreover, he followed the ANTI-CHRISTIAN bias of his master by using, in some passages interpreted Messianically by the Church, another word in place of *Christos* ('anointed') and in Isaiah 7:14 *neanis* ('young woman') instead of *parthenos* ('virgin'). (*Our Bible and the Ancient Manuscripts*, Sir F. Kenyon, 1958, p. 103)

F. Crawford Burkitt, who published these fragments (Number 7), does not draw the same conclusions as the WBTS. For instance, on p. 18 of his publication, *Fragments of the Book of Kings According to the Translation of Aquila*, he explains that one of the main tasks of scholars is to separate the pure from the mixture. He adds that this find is 'of very great importance for the textual study of the LXX' because it is a classic example of mixture!

He makes it even clearer:

> To the scribe of our MS the Tetragrammaton must have been a mere symbol, blindly copied from the model ... The Tetragrammaton in our MS was UNDOUBTEDLY INTENDED TO BE pronounced *kyrios* ... Contractions are extremely infrequent in our MS and when they occur they are always at the end of lines. The scribe, in fact, used contractions only to avoid dividing words. Now at the end of 4 Kgs. 23 24 [2 Kgs. 23:24 in our Bibles] ... there was no room to write the Tetragrammaton in full, so instead ... we find ... *ku*. The Greek Synagogue, therefore, READ THE NAME *KYRIOS*. (pp. 15-16)

The Society is deceptive in bringing this version in as evidence because it contains *kyrios* and shows just how the name was pronounced.

Number 9 – Sym[P.Vindob.G.39777]

This version by Symmachus was a revision of the Aquila text around AD 200, to meet the needs of a Jewish sect who were dissatisfied with the LXX.

Number 10 – Ambrosian 0 39 sup.

This is simply a compilation of various other versions and therefore adds no new evidence to the case.

The Chester Beatty Papyri

Before we summarise this section we need to underline another of the classic deceptions of the WBTS. Not only has it twisted the evidence it has presented, but also it has omitted evidence that disproves its point. Several manuscripts found in Egypt containing parts of the Old Testament in Greek, as well as parts of the New Testament, called 'The Chester Beatty Papyri,' were published under that name by F. G. Kenyon in 1937. All contain abbreviations of *theos* and *kyrios*, not the tetragram. What is even more remarkable is that the *Watchtower* quotes Kenyon's comments on these very papyri under *Insight*'s article on 'Manuscripts and the Bible'. 'The first and most important conclusion derived from the examination of them [the Papyri] is the satisfactory one that they confirm the essential soundness of the existing texts.' (*Insight*, Vol. 2, p. 318)

Conclusion

The evidence presented shows that some uncommon LXX versions contain the tetragram but we cannot conclude from this that all or even most do. In fact we read 'The LXX is characterized by the Hellenizing of Israelite-Jewish monotheism and by the reduction of the designations of God ... The name *Yahweh* or *Yah*, which is mostly translated by *kyrios*, is replaced by *theos* only about 330 times.' (*Dictionary of New Testament Theology*, 1971, Vol. 2, p. 70)

Most of the early versions of the LXX are of Jewish origin and the scribes were determined to keep old traditions. These have nothing to do with the work of the Christians in the New Testament.

Howard's theory

As we have been at pains to point out, Howard's work was only a theory. A cornerstone to this theory is the use of *'nomina sacra'* in the NT manuscripts. These are abbreviations of certain words such as *christos, kurios, theos*. Howard's theory is that these were directly influenced by the abbreviation of the divine name in the OT.

What is not presented to the Witness is the fact that C. H. Roberts in his book *Manuscript, Society and Belief in Early Christian Egypt*, argues very positively that this was not the case. He concludes quite clearly that the way the early Christian manuscripts were written showed no influence from the way the Hebrew manuscripts had been produced.

This alone shows that the WBTS can put no weight into a theory that it has turned into fact. What though is even more relevant, as we shall see later, is that if this theory were true then as Doug Mason concludes in Jehovah In The NWT,

> If the *nomina sacra* were of Jewish Christian origin as Roberts argues so convincingly for, and Howard fails to counter, then the Tetragram would have been removed by AD 50 or AD 70 at the latest, well before the NT was recognized as Scripture ... [and] all changes or decisions such as those regarding the Tetragram or the creation of the *nomina sacra*, would have been made by and under the control of the pure apostolic church. (p. 59)

Even accepting Howard's theory then it is impossible to argue, as we shall see that the Watchtower does, that the manuscripts were altered in the second or third centuries.

However, the *KIT*, p. 1137, actually claims to have another piece of evidence to prove that the tetragram appeared in the Christian Greek Scriptures. 'Matthew's Gospel account was first written in Hebrew rather than in Greek, as is indicated by Jerome, of the fourth and fifth centuries CE.'

The *KIT* account continues with Jerome's description of Matthew's Gospel in Hebrew. What it does not tell, or maybe does not know, is that in his work *Evangelium Secundum*, Jerome rejects this text as being the Gospel of Matthew and identifies it with the apocryphal work of the Gospel to the Hebrews. Early scholars thought that this or similar manuscripts were the original of the Gospel of Matthew but many modern scholars now reject this theory:

> It is generally not difficult to discover when a Gr.[eek] book of this period is a tr[anslation] from the Heb[rew] or the Aram[aic]. That our Mat[thew] was written originally in Gr[eek] appears, among other things, from the way in which it makes use of the O[ld] T[estament], sometimes following the LXX, sometimes going back to the Heb[rew]. (*International Standard Bible Encyclopaedia*, 1978, Vol. 3, p. 2010)

A greater problem

If the divine name has been removed from the Scriptures, why did God allow it? In addition, if He allowed it, has He ordained the Society to reverse the position? First, what does the Watchtower say itself about the New Testament Scriptures?

> But despite the variations peculiar to different manuscript families (and the variations within each group), the Scriptures have come down to us IN ESSENTIALLY THE SAME FORM AS THE ORIGINAL INSPIRED WRITINGS. The variations of reading are of no consequence as to Bible teachings in general. And scholastic collations have corrected ERRORS OF ANY IMPORTANCE, so that we enjoy an authentic and reliable text. (*Insight*, Vol. 2, p. 314)

> Appreciation of the reliability of the Bible is greatly enhanced when it is realized that, by comparison, there are only very few extant manuscripts of the works of classical secular writers and none of these are original, autograph manuscripts. Though they are only copies made centuries after the death of the authors, present-day scholars accept such late copies as sufficient evidence of the authenticity of the text... Manuscripts and versions of the Greek Christian Scriptures bear UNASSAILABLE TESTI-

MONY TO THE MARVELLOUS PRESERVATION AND ACCURATE TRANS-
MISSION OF THAT PORTION OF GOD'S WORD. (*Insight*, Vol. 2, pp.
317-8)

On the one hand, the Society accepts these manuscripts as
proof of the accuracy of God's Word today. But on the other, it
still insists that there have been major changes, with the tetragrammaton being replaced in hundreds of instances. (See
Insight, Vol. 2, pp. 7-8)

Conclusions

1. You cannot have it both ways. If Bible manuscripts are
   accurate then the name could not have been removed.
2. As already seen if it were removed it would have been mid-
   way through the first century AD and impossible to be during the second or third.

So, with the 'evidence' that the name was removed from the
New Testament shown to be non-existent, we must take a close
look at the scholarship of the Society which 'puts it back in'.

Scholarship

Anyone who has read the *KIT* or *NWT* will recognise 'J references' (indicated in the following text by J1, J2, etc.). These are
the translations cited by the Society as giving it authority to
'replace' the name of 'Jehovah' in the Greek Scriptures. But do
these translations really give such authority?

> J2, which was written 'AGAINST Christianity' was revised
> as 'J3' and later as 'J4'. J7 was revised as 'J8'' and later, in
> part, as 'J10'. The London Jewish Society (see Note 3)
> published J11, J13 and J16, while translators who helped
> prepare these publications also prepared J14 and J15.
> This demonstrates a degree of commonality between J11,
> J13, J14, J15 and J16. The extent of the Society's 'support'
> is reduced even further when it is recognized that only

nine of the nineteen Hebrew translations relate to the whole of the Greek Scriptures; included in these nine are J7 and J8 which are related, and also J11, J13, J14 and J16, which are also related. (Doug Mason, *Witnessing the Name*, 1981, p. 31)

This shows the weakness of the 'J' evidence, and it becomes further diluted when you discover that the oldest translation is 1385, the next 1537 and from there on up to 1981! Most are by Jewish authors who have a reason for putting the name back in.

The authority of these 'J' references is accepted above that of some of the oldest New Testament manuscripts. We will look at this in more detail presently, but first what does the WBTS say about these manuscripts?

Biblical papyri of GREAT IMPORTANCE were among papyrus codices found in Egypt about 1930 ... three contain portions of fifteen books of the Christian Greek Scriptures ... The international designation for Biblical papyri is a capital 'P' followed by a small number ... Quite noteworthy is P46. (*Insight*, Vol. 2, pp. 315-6)

Here though we discover the Society's deception. It will praise these manuscripts, of 'great importance,' but it will reject them over 250 times for insignificant works of biased men when replacing the name of Jehovah in the New Testament.

1 Cor. 7:17 is very significant, where all manuscripts are rejected in favour of no 'J's' (in 1950 the Watchtower said it was supported by J7 and J8, but does not today). If it had not made the change then the Lord Jesus would be equated with God.

There are times in the New Testament where it would be inappropriate, as far as the WBTS is concerned, to put 'Jehovah'. Here, all of a sudden, it accepts the original manuscripts over its 'J' translations. This has nothing to do with scholarship but the desire of the Society to put over its biased views. The following are some of the most notable that are worth pointing out to the Witnesses.

Rom. 10:9. J12-14, 16-18, 22 all contain the Hebrew phrase *ha'adhon* which the *NWT*, p. 1568, tells us is limited 'exclusively to Jehovah God.' But we find the translators prefer the manuscripts because they have 'Lord'.

1 Thess. 4:16-17. Three times here there is a change, so that Jesus' coming is not seen as Jehovah's coming. In verse 16 and the first instance in verse 17 – J7, 8, (13, 14) have 'Jehovah', and in the second instance of verse 17 – J7, 8, 13, 14, 24 have 'Jehovah'. This evidence was widely accepted before but now the *NWT* prefers the manuscripts.

2 Tim. 1:18. This must have given the translators a headache because 'the Lord is to grant mercy from the Lord.' There is no problem if you accept the biblical revelation of the Trinity but to the Watchtower, one must be the God, Jehovah and the other 'little god,' Jesus. A secondary problem also arises because, according to the Society's explanation of John 1:1, where the definite article *ho* is found, that must be the God Jehovah, and where it isn't found it is the 'little god' Jesus. Yet if you do that here it would appear that Jehovah is subservient to Jesus and so *ho kyrios* becomes the little god Jesus and *kyriou* becomes the God Jehovah. This clear twisting of its own teaching is in addition to the fact that *ho kyrios* in J7, 8, 13, 14, 16 is 'Jehovah' and the *kyriou* in J7, 8, 13, 14, 16-18, 22-24 is also 'Jehovah'. If the translators had been honest they would have had to translate this verse, 'May Jehovah grant him to find mercy from Jehovah in that day.'

1 Pet. 3:15. Probably this is the classic deliberate mistranslation. First it is an Old Testament quotation and therefore should be translated 'Jehovah'. Secondly, J7, 8, 11-14, 16, 17,24 all say 'Jehovah' and according to the Society's 'rules of translation' should have been chosen instead of the manuscripts. We would then read, 'But sanctify Jehovah as Lord in your hearts ... ', not , 'But sanctify the Christ as Lord in your hearts ... '

Rev. 16:5. J7, 8, 13, 14, 16 say, 'you, Jehovah,' but the Society prefers the 'You' of the manuscripts. However, we should read, 'You, Jehovah, the One who is and was ... '

Chapter 8 – Salvation

The basis for this section comes from two articles that first appeared in *Bethel Ministries Newsletters*, March/April 1986 & September/October 1989. They are used with the kind permission of R. Watters.

Did Jesus die on a cross?
The Society has made an issue of the shape of the cross and holds true to its pattern of majoring in minor issues. The Society considers the churches as 'unclean' for using the cross as a symbol of the death of Jesus. Certainly, worship of the cross or any other symbol is wrong, but the use of a symbol for illustrative purposes is not wrong?

Watchtower quotes
Until the late 1930's, the Society pictured Christ dying on the traditional cross. (See for example *The Harp of God*, 1921, p. 114.) Several *WT* magazines in the early 1900's pictured a cross on the front cover and one even told us the weight of the cross! (See *ZWTR*, 15 April 1913, p. 5221)

In 1936, the book *Riches* stated that Jesus was not crucified on a cross but on a tree. In 1937 Rutherford began making an issue of the cross, saying that Christ died on an upright stake, and that churches were corrupt for using a 'pagan' object as a centre of attention. In the book *Enemies*, he attacks the traditional story of the cross as wrong because 'The Cross was worshipped by the Pagan Celts long before the [birth] and death of Christ.' (pp. 188-89)

What pagans did with crosses before the death of Christ has nothing to do with how the Romans crucified people. Besides, Jesus did not choose his instrument of death.

The Society continues to use this argument today. *Reasoning*, p. 90, asks, 'What were the historical origins of Christendom's cross?' Its first quote, in answer, is from the *EB* Vol. 6, 1946, p. 753, but it misses out the following part:

> **The death of Christ on the cross necessarily conferred a new significance on the figure, which had hitherto been associated with a conception of religion not merely non-Christian but in essence often opposed to it.**

Indeed if the cross was not a pagan symbol it would be quite surprising because Jesus died a pagan death.

As years went by, 'proof' was supplied. In 1950, with the release of the NWT, the appendix (pp. 768-71) first argued that the Greek words *stauros* (Matt. 10:38) and *xylon* (Acts 5:30) do not mean a cross, and that these words only mean an upright stake without a crossbeam. It said that there is no proof to the contrary. A woodcut from a sixteenth-century book, *De Cruce Liber Primus* (corrected in 1984 to *De Cruce Libri Tres*), by Justus Lipsius, picturing a man on an upright stake is presented as, 'This is the manner in which Jesus was impaled.'

The Society makes this final point:

> The evidence is, therefore, completely lacking that Jesus Christ was crucified on two pieces of timber placed at a right angle. We refuse to add anything to God's written Word by inserting the pagan cross into the inspired Scriptures, but render *stauros* and *xylon* according to the simplest meanings... The passing of time and further archaeological discoveries will be certain to prove its cor-

rectness. Even now the burden rests upon all who contend for the religious tradition to prove that Jesus died on more than a simple stake.

Over the years further 'evidence' has been added and now the Society's objections consist of four major points:

1. The biblical Greek does not suggest a cross.
2. The cross was a pagan symbol later adopted by the 'apostate' church.
3. Archaeology proves that Jesus died on an upright stake rather than a cross.
4. The cross is to be shunned rather than mentioned or displayed.

What is the scholarly response to these claims?

What the Greek says
The Greek *stauros* has the primary meaning of a pole or stake but what the Society does not mention is that the word often refers to more complex constructions, such as the cross.

Authoritative lexicons give the definition of *stauros* as a 'stake sunk into the earth in an upright position; a cross-piece was often attached to its upper part'. (*A Greek-English Lexicon*, Arndt and Gingrich, p. 772). *The New International Dictionary of New Testament Theology* reads:

> Corresponding to the v[er]b (*stauroo*) which was more common, stauros can mean a stake ... *Stauros* could also be an instrument of torture, perhaps in the sense of the Lat[in] *patibulum*, a cross-beam laid on the shoulders. Finally it could be an instrument of execution in the form of a vertical stake and a cross-beam of the same length forming a cross in the narrower sense of the term ... The exact technical form and significance of execution are not conveyed by the words ... without further

definition... it is necessary to know in what region and under what authority the execution was carried out. It is also necessary to know the standpoint of the writer who uses the term. (Vol. 1, p. 391)

The Greek word *xylon* can mean 'wood, a piece of wood, or anything made of wood', and can refer to a cross as well, as pointed out in *Vine*, Vol. 4, p. 153.

Stauros and *xylon* can both be used to refer to a cross, a fact carefully side-stepped by the Society. We must therefore look to the historical record for decisive proof.

Historical and archaeological evidence for the cross

What the Society specifically ignores is that the Romans executed prisoners on a cross. The horizontal bar of such crosses was called the patibulum, and slaves to be executed were customarily made to carry the patibulum to the place of execution. (See *Biblical Quarterly*, Vol. 13, No. 4, p. 442)

Justus Lipsius

The apparent evidence from Justus Lipsius is actually deception. In editions of the *NWT* prior to 1984 it reproduced one illustration of a man impaled on an upright stake and failed to mention that there are fifteen other illustrations, most of which picture various crucifixions on crosses. After referring to this illustration, it states 'This is the manner on which Jesus was impaled.'

The deception continues when it states 'evidence is completely lacking' that Jesus was crucified on a cross, when this very book says that Jesus died on a cross! A partial translation from the Latin reads, 'In the Lord's cross there were four pieces of wood, the upright beam, the crossbar, a tree trunk (piece of wood) placed below, and the title (inscription) placed above.'

Where did Lipsius put this text? Next to the illustration of a crucifixion on a cross. Since the exposure of this dishonesty the Society was forced in publications from 1984 onwards to leave this statement out. Nevertheless, it still uses Lipsius's illustration of a stake and fails to tell the real story!

Recent archaeological finds
Some recent archaeological finds are very embarrassing for the Society. In earlier editions (1950 and 1969) of the *NWT* it wrote 'The passing of time and further archaeological discoveries will be certain to prove its correctness. Even now the burden rests upon all who contend for the religious tradition to prove that Jesus died on more than a simple stake.'

We will see why it has omitted this statement from the 1984 and 1985 versions of the *NWT*.

Buried History, Vol. 9, No. 2, p. 41, pictured a satirical graffito, dated shortly after AD 200, taken from the walls of the Roman Palatine. It depicted a crucified ass, which is intended as a mockery of a Christian prisoner who worships Christ. The Romans were no doubt amused that Christians worshipped this Jesus whom they had crucified on a cross.

In June 1968, bulldozers working north of Jerusalem accidentally laid bare tombs dating from the first century BC and the first century AD. Here they unearthed the first skeletal remains of a crucified man. The most significant factor is its dating to around the time of Christ. Mr Tzaferis, an Israeli (not a Christian) wrote an article in the January/February 1985 issue of the secular *Biblical Archaeological Review*. He commented on the method of crucifixion used in the time of Jesus:

> At the end of the first century BC, the Romans adopted crucifixion as an official punishment for non-Romans for certain limited transgressions. During this early period, a wooden beam known as a 'furca' or 'patibulum' was placed on the slave's neck and bound to his arms ... Later, the slave was also stripped and scourged, increasing both the punishment and the humiliation ... Following the beating, the horizontal beam was placed upon the condemned man's shoulders, and he began the

long, gruelling march to the execution site, usually out-side the city ... In order to prolong the agony, Roman executioners devised two instruments that would keep the victim alive on the cross for extended periods of time. One known as a 'sedile', was a small seat attached to the front of the cross ... Both Erenaeus and Justin Martyr describe the cross of Jesus as having five extremi-ties rather than four; the fifth was probably the sedile. (pp. 48-49)

Extensive descriptions like this can be found in the very books that the Society often quotes from. These are ignored and its Writing Department seems to look high and low to find one quote that appears to agree with its position. This deceives the average Jehovah's Witness because it appears to be presenting sound scholarship, and its conclusions are seldom if ever ques-tioned.

This is illustrated by the answer to the question, 'Why do Watch Tower publications show Jesus on a stake with hands over his head instead of on the traditional cross?' (*Reasoning*, p. 89). It quotes another publication and we have put back in the parts left out by the Society.

The Greek word rendered 'cross' in many modern Bible versions ('torture stake' in NW) is *stauros* ... The *Imperial Bible Dictionary* acknowledges this, saying: "The Greek word for cross, (*stauros*), properly signified a stake, an upright pole, or piece of paling, on which anything might be hung, or which might be used in impaling (fencing in) a piece of ground. **But a modification was introduced as the dominion and usages of Rome extended themselves through Greek-speaking coun-tries.** Even amongst the Romans the crux (from which our cross is derived) appears to have been originally an upright pole, **and always remained the more promi-nent part. But from the time that it began to be used** as an instrument of punishment, a traverse piece of wood was commonly added ... about the period of the Gospel Age crucifixion was usually accomplished by suspending the criminal on a cross piece of wood". (*Reasoning*, p. 89)

Reasoning, p. 91, then quotes other authorities to answer the question, 'What were the historical origins of Christendom's cross?' It quotes the opening of the book *The Cross in Ritual, Architecture, and Art* by G. S. Tyack to show that the cross was originally used in pagan worship. But it does not go on to quote **"In all this the Christians of the first age would have rejoiced, claiming it as a world-wide prophecy of the Cross of the Redeemer."** (p. 3)

The Worship of the Dead, by Colonel J. Garnier, is quoted next, as saying that the cross was a pagan symbol. But on p. 225 we read **"Sin crucified is Salvation, but it is only by one cross that the power to do so is obtained, and that cross is the cross of Christ."**

One final quote we will mention is from *A Short History of Sex-Worship* by H. Cutner:

> Various figures of crosses are found everywhere on Egyptian monuments and tombs, and are considered by many authorities as symbolical either of the phallus [a representation of the male sex organ] or of coition. **Baring-Gould is of the contrary opinion and refuses to identify the cross with the phallus ...** In Egyptian tombs the *crux ansata* [cross with a circle or handle on top] is found side by side with the phallus. **The question of their connection is still hotly disputed. That the cross was a sacred sign long before Christ is supposed to have died upon one is conceded by Baring-Gould, for he believes that the cross 'formed a portion of that primeval religion, traces of which exist before the whole world among every people'.**

Chapter 12 – 1914 then and now

Chronology

What is chronology? The Chronological Institute was founded in London in 1852 and its aims included 'To promote ... a more comprehensive acquaintance with chronological litera-ture, and a more exact study of THIS SCIENCE, both historically and mathematically...' The definitions of chronology in the *EA, Oxford English Dictionary* and *Webster's International Dictionary* confirm that it is a science.

In contrast to these definitions, however, the complex chronology of the Watchtower is anything but scientific. Interestingly, its chronology did not begin with Russell at all.

> ... much of this parable [the ten virgins] met its fulfil-ment in 1843 and 1844, when William Miller and others, Bible in hand, walked out by faith on its statements, expecting Jesus at that time ... We merely notice here that the Bible chronology, first dug from Scripture by Bowen, of England ... Brother Barbour first began to preach the message... If these movements were of God, and if Bros. Miller and Barbour were his instruments ... the 'Bridegroom came' in 1874. (*ZWTR*, October and November 1881, pp. 288-89)

Russell accepted dates that had been fixed before him. He sim-ply 'juggled around' with starting and finishing points to arrive at a date that had not already passed.

John Aquila Brown seems to have been the first to use the figure of 2520 years (see later in this section) for the 'Gentile Times.' For Brown this ended in 1844. William Miller was an American influenced by the British school of chronology. He predicted the return of Christ during the Jewish year of 21 March 1843 to 21 March 1844.

Nelson H. Barbour, an associate of Miller, was severely disappointed at this failed prophecy but rechecked Miller's calculations against the work of the Revd Christopher Bowen and corrected them to make 1874 as the date for Christ's return. Russell accepted these calculations and claimed they were of God, but many changes were still to come. When Christ did not return visibly in 1874, it was said He came invisibly but that He would end all things and set up His kingdom on earth in 1914. Later the 1874 date was dropped altogether and Christ did not come invisibly until 1914.

Russell even used the Pyramid as proof of these dates.

> Then measuring down the 'Entrance Passage' ... we find it to be 3,416 inches, symbolizing 3,416 years from the above date, BC 1542. This calculation shows AD 1874 as marking the beginning of the period of trouble ... (*The Time is at Hand*, WBTS, 1901, p. 342)

When the Society changed the dates the pyramid seems to have stretched!

> Then measuring down the 'Entrance Passage' ... we find it to be 3,457 inches, symbolizing 3,457 years from the above date, BC 1542. This calculation shows AD 1915 as marking the beginning of the period of trouble ... (*The Time is at Hand*, WBTS, 1923, p. 342)

In all the chronology of the Society 1914 seems to be the one common theme, even though it has a different meaning today as the next chapter will show. First, what has a Jehovah's Witness been taught?

> Two dates are fixed with considerable certainty ... the beginning of the reign of Cyrus in 536 BC [see Note 1] ... (this) is a very important aid; for the Bible chronology ends with the '70 years desolation of the land,' ... the Bible alone, supplies such a chronology as the people of

God can rely upon ... Why not believe that God intended thus to provide a chronology as long as it was needed-down to the point where secular history could be depended upon as accurate [the Society would not agree with that today!] ... We do so believe. (*ZWTR*, 15 May 1896, p. 1975)

The Society has always seen the usefulness of chronology to promote its message of impending doom. Today the Society still uses chronology to establish the vital date of 1914, but does not accept all chronology, only parts that confirm its teaching. This can be seen clearly in the article on 'Chronology' (*Insight*, Vol. 1, pp. 447-467), where eleven pages are spent dismissing as inaccurate Egyptian, Assyrian, Babylonian and Persian historical records, astronomical calculations, archaeological dating and contemporary historians. Then it says ' ... we must use ... a date in history that has SOUND BASIS for acceptance ... as a pivotal point is the year 539 BCE, supported by VARIOUS HISTORICAL SOURCES.' (*Insight*, Vol. 1, p. 458)

The first calculation
Before we can check the accuracy of the Watchtower's chronology, we reproduce a number of quotes that sum up the steps taken in Watchtower chronology.

An absolute date is a calendar date that is proved by secular history to be the actual date of an event recorded in the Bible ... A prominent event recorded both in the Bible and in pagan secular history is the overthrow of ... Babylon ... October 11-12, 539 BCE. (*All Scripture Is Inspired Of God And Beneficial*, 1963, pp. 281-82)

Once this absolute date is fixed, calculations forward or backward from this date are made from accurate records in the Bible itsel f... the Bible record shows ... by late in 538 BCE Cyrus acceded to the throne, and ... at least before spring of 537 BCE, he issued his famous edict ... This would give ample opportunity for the Jews ... to come up to Jerusalem ... about October 1, 537 BCE. (*All Scripture Is Inspired Of God And Beneficial*, 1963, pp. 281-82)

With the exit of the insubordinate Jews from the land of Judah, the foretold 70 years of desolation of the land without resident Israelite and domesticated beast started off. (*WT*, 1 March 1980, p. 16)

About two lunar months after the calamity upon King Zedekiah his realm, the land of Judah, became totally desolated. There the 'seven times' of the nations, 'the times of the Gentiles', began their run of 2,520 years, to end in 1914 CE. (*WT*, 1 February 1980, p. 26)

There is no basis for doubt that Nebuchadnezzar's dream [Dan. 4] of the heaven-high tree was prophetic ... (it) symbolized the UNIVERSAL SOVEREIGNTY of ... Jehovah God ... True to that dream, Divine Sovereignty as exercised through the line of Davidic kings ... toppled ... in 607 BCE ... For how long was this debased appearance of Jehovah's Universal Sovereignty to continue? For 'seven times', which were prophetically illustrated by the 'seven years' of Nebuchadnezzar's dethronemen t... A 'time '... used in connection with Bible prophecy averaged 360 days ... The 'seven times' or seven years would therefore amount to 7 times 360 days, or 2,520 days. (*Our Incoming World Government – God's Kingdom*, 1977, pp. 83-84, 86-87; emphasis in the original)

So each of these 2,520 days must be treated according to the Bible rule: 'A day for a year, a day for a year, is what I give you' (Ezekiel 4:6; compare Numbers 14:34). This would mean that the 'seven times' of domination on the earth by Gentile world powers ... would extend for 2,520 years ... 607 BCE ... to ... 1914. (*Our Incoming World Government – God's Kingdom*, 1977, p. 88)

We will now look at each step in detail and check the accuracy of them.

Step 1: The absolute date

To date an event with a 'BC' date you must accept scientific chronology. The Society will say that it is using biblical chronology, but that only places events in their right order with the correct interval of years in between. The article in *WT*, 15 August 1968, entitled *The Book of Truthful, Historical Dates*, shows that it must use secular historians to establish the absolute date of 539 BC. It quotes twenty-five reliable authorities to fix 539 BC but at least twenty-two of these also prove that Jerusalem fell in 586/587 BC, not 607 BC as claimed by the Watchtower.

If these authorities are reliable over 539 BC, surely they are reliable over 586 BC? In any case, why choose 539 BC as the starting point when we could equally use 586 BC as the absolute date and be able to miss out the first two calculations? Sound scholarship would mean that we must either accept both 539 BC and 586 BC as reliable or reject both; they stand or fall together.

This is further shown by the basis for fixing 539 BC. The Watchtower article mentioned above explains ' ... a stone document ... (which) gives precise details ... This, in turn, enables modern scholars, with their knowledge of astronomy, to translate these dates into terms of the Julian or Gregorian calendars.' (p. 490)

On the same basis we can fix the absolute date for the fall of Jerusalem as 586 BC. This is based on a clay tablet with precise details that can be translated into terms of our modern-day calendar by the same accurate astronomical tables used for 539 BC.

The Society must have realised it was skating on thin ice

because a few years after the article in the Watchtower it changed its mind. '... the co-relation of astronomical data with human events in the past is subject to various factors and human interpretation, allowing for error.' (*Insight*, Vol. 1, p. 454) This means that 539 BC is not an absolute date and there is no reliable Watchtower chronology!

Step 2: From 539 to 537 BC
Once 539 BC is accepted, Jehovah's Witnesses will proudly tell you that only the Bible is used to establish the chronology. The first step then is to get from 539 to 537 BC. This is the two years between the fall of Babylon and the decree of Cyrus allowing the captives to return to Jerusalem. Where are these years mentioned in the Bible? The answer is nowhere! Even the Society agrees. '... IT IS VERY PROBABLE that the decree was made by the winter of 538 or toward the spring of 537.' (*Insight*, Vol. l, p. 458)

There is not enough information in the Bible about the events of the fall of Babylon to Darius the Mede and when Cyrus took over as ruler. Starting from 539 BC and using the Bible alone, all we could say is that the people returned to the land somewhere between 538 and 536 BC.

Step 3: Seventy years of desolation
The Watchtower is adamant that 70 years of complete desolation took place after the fall of Jerusalem in 607 BC. The Society's article on *Chronology* reads,

> From 607 BCE to return from exile. The length of this period is fixed by God's own decree concerning Judah, that 'all this land must become a devastated place, an object of astonishment, and these nations will have to serve the king of Babylon seventy years' – Jer. 25:8-11. The Bible prophecy does not allow for the application of this 70-year period to any time other than between the desolation of Judah... and the return of the Jewish exiles

to their homeland ... The prophet Daniel so understood the prophecy, for he states: 'I myself, Daniel, discerned by the books the number of the years concerning which the word of Jehovah had occurred to Jeremiah the prophet, for fulfilling the devastations of Jerusalem, namely, seventy years' (Dan. 9:2) ... 2 Chronicles 36:20,21 states: 'Furthermore, he carried off those remaining from the sword captive to Babylon ... to fulfil Jehovah's word by the mouth of Jeremiah, until the land had paid off its sabbaths' ... Jerusalem ... fell in... Nebuchadnezzar's 19th year of actual rule (counting from his accession year in 625 BC) ... However, 'some of the lowly people of the land' were allowed to remain... they fled into Egypt, finally leaving Judah completely desolate (2 Kings 25:9-12,22-26). This was in the seventh month ... Hence the count of the seventy years of desolation must have begun about October 1, 607 BCE ending in 537 BCE. (*Insight*, Vol. 1, p. 463)

In this article, both Daniel and the Chronicler refer to the prophecy of Jeremiah. In fact, all that was revealed about the seventy years came from Jeremiah. We will see what that is in just a moment but first we look at the question of whether the land was totally desolate without man and beast for seventy years.

Some Scriptures indicate that there was always a remnant within the land. Is. 6:11-13, for instance, talks about a land 'utterly desolate' but there was still a 'tenth portion' in it. Ezra 3:3 records when the altar was first set up because of the fear of the people in 'those countries'. Ezra 4:1, along with the annals of Esar-haddon, now in the British Museum, tell us that these were the people settled in the land from Babylon after the deportation of the Jews. Scripture gives evidence that this land was never completely without inhabitants and it did not need to be for it to have its 'sabbaths.' When the Jews were obeying

God's law and were keeping the sabbath year they did not leave the land but simply did not work the land.

This shows some of the misunderstanding of the seventy years by the Watchtower but there is another point that shows conclusively that it cannot use the seventy years to fill the gap from 607 to 537. This is the starting point of the seventy years. According to the Society the seventy years began in the nineteenth year of the reign of Nebuchadnezzar, which it relates to 607 BC.

The term 'seventy years' appears six times in Scripture, three times in Jeremiah; once in Daniel; once in Zechariah and once in 2 Chron. 36:21 dealing with the sabbaths. Having dealt with this last point already, we will look at the other references.

Jer. 25:11,12. This message came in the first year of Nebuchadnezzar (25:1). For twenty-three years, the Lord had spoken against the inhabitants of Jerusalem and His patience had run its course (v. 3). Now the Lord says 'I will bring the King of Babylon against you' (v. 9). After preaching the same message for twenty-three years without response and now telling the people what would happen do you think the Lord would wait another eighteen years (until Nebuchadnezzar's nineteenth year) to fulfil the judgement? Probably not. However, this as yet is not conclusive by itself.

Jer. 29:10. When Jeremiah spoke he was still in Jerusalem but some had already been taken captive to Babylon (v. 1). 'For thus says the Lord, "When seventy years have been completed for Babylon, I will visit you and fulfil My good word to you, to bring you back to this place."' (v.10).

Jeremiah was talking about the seventy years having already started, before the final destruction of Jerusalem. This is proof that the seventy years cannot start from that destruction. Do other Scriptures support this?

Dan. 9:2. Daniel mentions the desolations of Jerusalem. In the Watchtower's chronology article it mentions one group being taken captive at the destruction of Jerusalem, but Daniel mentions at least two desolations or devastations. The Society's article on Nebuchadnezzar (*Insight*, Vol. 2, p. 480), mentions that Nebuchadnezzar comes to Jerusalem earlier, when quoting from the Babylonian Chronicles. 'In this his ascension year he returned to Hattu and ... he took the vast booty of Hattu to Babylon.'

Hattu is Judah and this becomes clear when the Chronicles mention the destruction of Jerusalem, [Hattu]. Nebuchadnezzar, on the Society's own admission had been to Jerusalem before and taken away booty in his first or ascension year, the very year in which Jeremiah made the prophecy. Daniel expected the seventy years to be tied in with the devastations of Jerusalem, that is, the period would start from its first devastation, but from where did he draw this conclusion? Jeremiah the prophet. We therefore need to go back to Jer. 25:11,12 to see what led Daniel to that conclusion. 'These nations will serve the king of Babylon seventy years.'

Jeremiah did not prophesy, and therefore Daniel could not deduce, that the seventy years would start when Jerusalem fell. He said, and Daniel understood correctly, that the seventy years would begin when Jerusalem first came under the servitude of the King of Babylon. History and the Bible tell us that this was in the first year of his reign, not his nineteenth and so the seventy years, even according to Watchtower dating, must have begun around 590 BC. It is only by ignoring historical evidence and, even worse, by ignoring God's Word that the Society can conclude that the seventy years began with the fall of Jerusalem in 607 BC.

Step 4: 'The Times of the Gentiles'
The dream of Nebuchadnezzar recorded in Dan. 4 is the basis of this calculation. According to the Society, the tree in the dream represents 'divine rulership ... through the kingdom of

Judah' and the seven periods that elapsed after it was cut down are the 'Gentile Times'. The kingdom being restored to Nebuchadnezzar after these seven periods represents the Lord Jesus taking His seat on the throne vacated by King Zedekiah.

Unlike other dreams recorded in Daniel, the fulfilment of this one is also recorded. It is not for the 'end times', as others are. The word used for 'fulfilled' in verse 33 means 'to have an end of.' The tree represents Nebuchadnezzar, the king of Babylon, which is difficult to equate with the understanding of the Society that it represents divine rulership. 'What was really meant was ... domination exercised by the kingdom of God.' (*Babylon the Great has Fallen*, 1963, p. 177)

It is a foolish man that seeks to correct God.

Luke 21:24 mentions the 'Time of the Gentiles' and explains that during this time Jerusalem will be trampled down. That could not possibly have ended in 1914, but the Jehovah's Witness will try to wriggle out of this by saying it was the heavenly Jerusalem that was trampled down until 1914. However, the trampling started on earth and therefore must finish there. Is it anyway scriptural to say that the heavens were trampled down until 1914? See Eph. 1:20-23 (past tense in AD 60!).

According to the dating of the Society, Daniel was taken to Babylon in 617 BC (see Note 2) and the fall of Jerusalem was ten years later in 607 BC. In addition, this dream is a prophecy concerning the fall of Jerusalem. However, these two statements cannot be reconciled. The dream indicated a future event, to take place at least one year later (Dan. 4:29). If that event is the fall of Jerusalem, then the dream must have been received at the latest in 608 BC. That is impossible because the dream in Dan. 4 must come after the dream in Dan. 2 (compare 2:48 with 4:9). The Watchtower dates Dan. 2 (albeit falsely) as 605 BC, two years after the fall of Jerusalem.

The word for 'time' here is only found eleven times in the Old Testament and all are in the Book of Daniel. It is against sound biblical exegesis to isolate this one instance and compare it with Scriptures in Revelation, no matter how logical it appears. Daniel speaks of seven 'times'; these were times when there was no king of Israel ruling. Instead, God's people were dominated by a foreign power that did not recognise the God of the Jews. Rev. 12:6,14 shows another time of great testing for the people of God where three and a half 'times' equals 1260 days. This translates into the fact that seven 'times' equals 2520 days. Revelation is talking about another specific period of trouble for God's people that lasts seven years. This, of course, is not long enough for the Society, and therefore has to be linked with the next step.

Step 5: Day-years
The Society needs to transfer days into years and call upon the 'year for each day' theory, or, as it says, a 'Bible rule.' Edmund Gruss deals with this matter in detail in his book *The Jehovah's Witnesses and Prophetic Speculation*. In summary, here we will note that this 'rule' actually appears only twice in Scripture. The first time is in Num. 14:34 which speaks of the guilt of the children of Israel; they spied out the Promised Land for forty days but still disobeyed God and would not enter. They would therefore bear the guilt for forty years – a year for every day. The second example is Ezek. 4:6 which speaks again of the guilt of God's people. Ezekiel was a 'visual aid' for forty days – a day for every year.

There is no historical or biblical evidence to use a calculation of 2520 years as the period of the 'Gentile Times'. In addition, both Scriptures called on to turn days into years speak of the same matter, the guilt of God's people. The rule is not general but specific. In any case, the verses do not say the same thing: Num. 14:34 is a year for a day but Ezek. 4:6 is a day for a year.

Summary
1. The fall of Jerusalem in 607 BC is disproved by scientific chronology.
2. The date of 586 BC for the fall of Jerusalem is established both by scientific and biblical chronology.

3. Starting from an absolute date of 539 BC it is impossible, solely using the biblical record, to show that Jerusalem fell in 607 BC.
4. The way the WBTS uses Scripture is not sound interpretation but a taking of individual passages at random to prove a point that has been determined beforehand.
5. The result of these conclusions is that 1914 is not proven as the significant date of Christ's invisible return.

Note 1

It is interesting to note that the WBTS has had three other 'absolute dates' before 539 BC but because of minor changes in the way it calculated the Gentile Times these could always end at AD 1914.

> ... the first year of the reign of Cyrus is a very clearly fixed date-both secular and religious histories with marked unanimity agreeing with Ptolemy's Canon, which places it BC 536. (*The Divine Plan of the Ages*, WBTS, 1889, p. 80)

> According to the most accurate histories ... Cyrus came to power in 537 BC. (*The Kingdom is at Hand*, WBTS, 1944, p. 183)

> The first year of Cyrus ... 538 BC. (*WT*, 1 November 1949, p. 326)

Note 2

> Early in 617 BCE ... Daniel ... [was] taken ... by Nebuchadnezzar. (*Insight*, Vol. 1, p. 576)

> Ezekiel ... was ... taken to Babylon by Nebuchadnezzar with Jehoiachin in 617 BCE. (*Insight*, Vol. 1, p. 91)

The Society says that Ezekiel and Daniel were taken captive in the same year thus ruling out Nebuchadnezzar coming to Jerusalem in his first year. Whereas this makes it impossible for the seventy years to start then, it does cause other problems.

1. Dan. 1:3-4 tells us that when Daniel was taken it was not a general exile. Just a few of the 'elite' were taken to the palace.
2. Daniel does not mention king Jehoiachin but Ezekiel does. It would be strange not to report the king being taken to the palace.
3. If Daniel was not taken to Babylon until 617 BC, how could he interpret Nebuchadnezzar's dream in the second year of the king (Dan. 2:1) which according to the Watchtower is 624/23 BC?

Note 3
The original title of this group is probably *The London Society for the Promotion of Christianity among the Jews*, normally shortened to London Jewish Society. Today it is known as *The Church's Ministry among the Jews*.

Appendix A –
The Bible study
— ∽ —

Introduction

Leaving the WBTS is usually a traumatic experience. You will sever contact with many friends and have restricted contact with close family.

Another cause for concern might be your eternal security. You have been taught that the only way to escape God's judgement is to belong to the Watchtower, and if you leave you wonder if you will forfeit this right. We want you to know that there are those who understand what you are going through.

Some will find the following questions adequate in themselves whereas others will want personal help. If you are one of these, please contact us and we will try to put you in touch with someone locally. Failing a personal contact, we will certainly arrange for someone to write to you.

The aim of these questions is to show scriptural answers to the errors that you have been taught in the past. We will try not to force preconceived ideas on you but simply ask questions and allow you to dig the answers from the Bible.

Up until now, you have been dependent on the Society as 'the servant giving food in due season,' and we do not want to replace them with another man or society. The Bible shows that the main source of 'spiritual food' is a personal relationship with the Lord, which is supplemented and indeed safeguarded by the corporate meetings of the church.

We recommend, because of mistranslations in the *New World*

Translation, that you use a version such as the *New American Standard Bible*.

Lesson 1: The open Book

Acts 17:11
1. What did the Bereans study to check Paul's teaching?
2. What should we study to check the teaching we hear?

2 Tim. 3:16-17
3. Who is made adequate and equipped for every good work?
4. Does this description only apply to a few of God's people?
5. What are the Scriptures profitable for?

1 Cor. 2:9-16
6. Who, according to verse 9, will receive things that have been hidden up until now?
7. Is this you?
8. How does God reveal things to us?
9. Who, according to verses 14 and 15, can receive God's Word?
10. What makes a man or woman spiritual? Does belonging to a particular society? Doing good works? Receiving God's Holy Spirit?

1 Tim. 2:4
11. Who does God desire to come to the knowledge of the truth?

Summary questions
A. Who can understand the Bible?
B. How can we understand the Bible?
C. Has God restricted the understanding of the Bible to just a few?

Lesson 2: Receiving food

Josh. 1:8
1. What was Joshua to do?
2. What does it mean to meditate?
3. Was Joshua to meditate on God's Word or a book about God's Word?
4. What was the result of meditating?

I Cor. 10:3,11 and Exod. 16:4-36
5. Should we learn from the mistakes they made in the Old Testament?
6. Did the children of Israel get their food from Moses?
7. Did Jehovah show any favouritism as to who should get the most?
8. Did God's supply to the people ever run out?
9. According to Exod. 16:4, what did the people need to do?

Col. 3:16
10. Whose Word should dwell within us?
11. In what measure?
12. Does the Word affect just our minds?
13. What should I read often to fulfil this verse?

Summary questions
A. Who do we receive our food from?
B. Should we receive our food weekly, daily, or when?
C. Which part of us should be full of God's Word?

Lesson 3: The Kingdom and its gospel

Eph. 1:18-23
1. When was Christ enthroned in heaven?
2. Is there a gap between His ascension and His enthronement?

John 18:36-37
3. Is Christ's kingdom like other kingdoms of this world?
4. Was Jesus already King of His kingdom at this time?

Col. 1:13
5. What had Paul been delivered from?
6. What had Paul been delivered into?
7. Can this be our experience?

Rev. 21:23-26 and 22:4
8. Is the New Jerusalem the 'capital' city of the kingdom?
9. Will others be going into the city, besides those who live there?
10. Will they see the Lord Jesus?
11. Does this mean that the New Heavens and the New Earth are blended together?

1 Cor. 15:1-4
12. Do these verses summarise the gospel of the kingdom that Paul preached?
13. What are the three main aspects of this gospel?

Col. 1:25-29
14. What was Paul's God-given task?
15. Was this for a few people or all people?
16. Can you benefit from this same preaching today?

Summary questions
A. When was Christ enthroned as King?
B. Is the kingdom for all or a few?
C. How can I live in the good of Christ's kingdom reign?

Lesson 4: Born again

John 10:15-16
1. Who does Christ lay down His life for?

2. Remembering who Jesus is talking to, who do you think the 'other sheep' are?
3. How many flocks (classes) do we end up with?
4. Do we all have the same experience of the Lord?

1 John 5:1
5. Who is born of God?
6. Is this restricted to a certain number?

2 Cor. 5:17
7. What happens to our past when we experience this new life in Christ?

John 14:23
8. Who does Jesus say will live with us in our new life?
9. Is this a physical or spiritual dwelling with us?

John 3:3
10. What needs to happen to us if we want to see Christ's kingdom?
11. According to the following Scriptures, what must I do to be born again?
    Rom. 3:23 – What must I realise?
    Rom. 6:23 – What must I realise?
    1 John 5:11-13 and **John 1:12**
    Rom. 10:9-10

Summary questions
A. Is being born again an experience for just a few people?
B. Can I be born again?
C. How can I be born again?

Lesson 5: Death and judgement

1 Thess. 5:23
1. How many parts is man made up from?

2. Will all of them be preserved at the Lord's coming?

Heb. 12:22-23
3. Where were the spirits of these men who had died?
4. Does everyone's 'spirit' go to heaven at death?

Matt. 10:28
5. Can a natural man kill the soul as well as the body?
6. Who alone has the ability to destroy the soul?
7. Are the body and the soul made and destroyed in the same way?

2 Cor. 5:6-9
8. For Paul, would there be any waiting to be with the Lord when he left the body?
9. When he was at home with the Lord was he absent from 'body, soul and spirit', 'body and soul', or 'body'?

Heb. 9:27-28
10. When does our judgement come?
11. Does this verse (or indeed any other) teach that we have a second chance after death?
12. When Christ returns will He still be dealing with the sins of His people?

Summary questions
A. According to the Bible does the soul return to dust?
B. According to the Bible does our spirit go straight to heaven when we die?
C. According to the Bible do we have a 'second chance' to pass God's judgement after we have died?

Lesson 6: Jehovah-Jesus-Holy Spirit

Deut. 6:4
1. How many 'Gods' are there?

2. Why do you think the Hebrew word for God is the plural word *Elohim*? Compare Deut. 4:31: 'the Lord your God (plural – *Elohim*) is a compassionate God (singular – *El*).

John 6:27
3. Who is God according to this verse?

John 20:28
4. Who is God according to this verse?

Acts 5:3-4
5. Who did Ananias lie to according to verse 3?
6. Who did Ananias lie to according to verse 4?
7. Therefore, who is God according to these verses?
8. The Bible says there is only one God. But it also declares that three people are that God. How can this be explained?

Gal. 1:1
9. Who raised Jesus from the dead?
10. Now read **John 2:19-21**. Who raised Jesus from the dead here?
11. Can two separate people raise Jesus from the dead? If not what is the explanation?

Summary questions
A. Does the Bible teach that there is more than one God?
B. Does the Bible teach that Jehovah is God?
C. Does the Bible teach that Jesus is God?
D. Does the Bible teach that the Holy Spirit is God?
E. Overall then, what does the Bible teach concerning Jehovah, Jesus and the Holy Spirit?

Lesson 7: Faith and works

Eph. 2:8-10
1. How are we saved?

2. Are good works essential for our salvation?
3. Why does God not allow works to count towards our salvation?
4. Are the good works that we do of our own choosing?

Rom. 4:1-5
5. How was Abraham justified?
6. In the light of verse 4, can we work to receive the reward of eternal life?
7. Why, according to verse 5, is it more important to have faith than works?

John 6:28-29
8. What is the most important work for us to do?

James 2:14-26
9. According to verses 14 and 15, who is James talking to?
10. In the light of **Eph. 2:8-9**, is James talking about initial salvation, that is, being born again, or about our continual growth into the fullness of our salvation?
11. In the light of **Rom. 4:1-5** is James talking about initial salvation, that is, being born again, or about our continual growth into the fullness of our salvation?
12. Can we be a growing Christian and not display God's works that He has prepared?
13. What are the works that God has prepared for you to do?

Summary questions
A. Are works necessary for us to be born again?
B. How does the Bible teach us we can be saved (born again)?
C. As the Bible does not contradict itself, how do you explain **James 2:14-26** in the light of **Eph. 2:8-9**?

Appendix B –
Books, tapes and videos

— ⌒ —

Books

The Truth Revealed – photocopies of Watchtower errors and discrepancies. Plus some helpful witnessing tips. **Q**

An Alternative View – Fourteen sheets containing a different doctrine of the Jehovah's Witnesses with clear Biblical explanations of how to answer them.

Watch the Tower – A compilation of the errors, mistakes and deliberate changes in the literature of the WBTS. **Q**

The Name above all Names – A Biblical investigation into the Watchtower teaching on the importance of the 'name of Jehovah'. Especially produced for you to present to the Jehovah's Witness.

Why should you believe 'Should you Believe in the Trinity'? – This is written to be a clear answer to the Watchtower booklet on the Trinity. Shows clearly the dishonest scholarship of the Society on this issue. **Q**

Examining the Watchtower Bible – A sixteen-page investigation into the mistranslation of the *New World Translation*. **Q**

Crisis of Conscience – The author, Ray Franz, was a member of the Governing Body of Jehovah's Witnesses for nine years. Here he reveals the struggle he faced in coming to terms with the fact that the WBTS was not God's chosen organisation.

Cassette tapes

Who's There – A double tape set (includes one on the Mormons.) In a discussional style with a former member we discover what it was like to be a Jehovah's Witness, what they believe and we actually act out conversations we can have with them. **Q**

Where are the 'great crowd'?, Jehovah's Witness Doctrines, New World Mistranslation, and *Jehovah's Witnesses and salvation* – Four cassettes, each with an in-depth examination of an area of concern.

Videos

Reach out to Jehovah's Witnesses – A documentary style presentation of who they are, what they believe and how to witness to them. **Q**

Awake! to the Watchtower – two videos in four parts, that explain why we should bother to witness to Jehovah's Witnesses, what they believe and how to talk to them, in seminar form.

Jehovah's Witnesses and salvation – An in depth look at the subject.

Witnesses of Jehovah – Documentary presentation of what the WBTS really is.

Jehovah's Witnesses: A non-profit organization – An examination of the WBTS's own account of its history.

All the above resources are available from Reachout Trust. Call 0181 332 7785 for latest prices and availability. Orders accepted over the phone when paid for by Visa or Mastercard.

Q = Resource includes 'Questions to ask' as explained on p. 202

Appendix C – The Reachout Trust

— ⟡ —

What Reachout does

Reachout Trust is an international Christian ministry that upholds biblical truth and builds bridges to people in the cults, occult, and New Age. Its primary aim is reaching out to the people involved in these groups. This is achieved through various means:

- Training Christians to be effective witnesses to people involved.
- Providing relevant teaching and resource material for use in training and witnessing.
- Providing advisers for people wishing to leave the group they are involved in.
- Providing a general information service on the cults, occult and new age.

If you need further help or have an interesting story to tell please contact us. We will do all we can to be of service to you. If you want help on a more personal level, we would arrange for an advisor to contact you.

All the resources listed in Appendix B are available from Reachout Trust, please contact us (details on p. 253) for up-to-date prices. We accept orders over the telephone paid for via Visa or Mastercard.

If you feel able to help in any of the ways described in this section or if you need help please tick the appropriate box on the Response Form on p. 253.

What you can do for Reachout

Reachout Team. Responsible Christians are needed in all parts of Britain to become part of the Reachout Team. This could mean being a Regional Coordinator; an Area Director; a helper on particular projects; an adviser or carer to those wanting to leave the group they are involved in or the families of those involved.

Reachout registration. Your church could register with the Trust. We need churches that are willing and able to look after those on their way out of a group.

Quarterly Mailings. You could help send out these. We would send you labels in multiples of fifty, plus the enclosures. You would need to purchase envelopes, 11 x 22 cm, insert and post. At current postage rates, this works out at approximately £10 per fifty addresses.

Regular prayer times are vital to the work. Would you be willing to arrange one in your area once a month?

What can Reachout do for you?

Reachout Quarterly. A magazine full of helpful articles on many cults, occult and New Age groups. It keeps you up to date with the situation in this country and has some interesting snippets from abroad. There are also special offers only available to *Quarterly* readers. We do not charge for this service but donations are welcomed.

Regular giving. Would you or your church be willing to give a regular small amount to the work of the Trust? A number of different giving schemes are available.

Seminars. We would welcome the opportunity to arrange one of our seminars in your church. The teaching in these seminars is vital for Christians to be prepared to understand and help those caught up in these groups.

Training Days and Annual Convention. These are special times in the Reachout calendar not to be missed. Be sure to ask for all the latest details.

Aims
Reachout Trust will:

- Examine in the light of the Christian gospel the beliefs and spirituality of people within the cults, occults, New Age and all not upholding biblical truth.
- Train and equip Christians to explain the Christian gospel in a relevant way.
- Provide a complete service of advice and help to all enquirers.
- Present the Christian gospel.
- Work with organisations which will help achieve these aims.

Statement of Faith
All associated with Reachout Trust are asked to agree to the following:

- The unity, equality and individual personality of the Father, the Son, and the Holy Spirit, in the Godhead.
- God is the Father of all those who fully believe in the Lord Jesus Christ.

- The Lord Jesus Christ is the only begotten, not created, Son of God. Redeemer for all mankind, and the one Mediator between God and man. He is also coming again to earth.
- The vital need for the Holy Spirit to dwell in every believer and lead him or her into the reality of Christ's completed work.
- The sinful state all men and the necessity for everyone to experience New Birth.
- The whole Bible is the divinely inspired Word of God and it has absolute authority in all matters of faith and conduct.

Index

— ໑ —

249

Response Form

Please use BLOCK LETTERS on this form. Photocopy this page to avoid damaging the book before returning to the address below:

Title: Mr Mrs Ms Miss Rev _____ (Please circle or add other title)

Name: _____

Address: _____

_____

Postcode: _____ Telephone: _____

Requests:
❑ Please send me a full information pack on Reachout Trust
❑ Please send me the *Reachout Quarterly*
❑ Please send me details of training days/annual convention
❑ Please send me details of your giving schemes

Offers of help
❑ I might arrange a seminar in our church
❑ I would like to be part of the Reachout Team
❑ I would like to register my church with Reachout
❑ I would like to despatch mailings each quarter
❑ I would like to arrange a regular prayer meeting

Please send this form to:
Reachout Trust
24 Ormond Road
Richmond Surrey TW10 6TH
Tel: 0181 332 7785 fax: 0181 332 0286
e-mail: awake@reachouttrust.org

Be sure to check out our web site: